FELTED KNITS

Beverly Galeskas

EDITOR Lorrie LeJeune
TECHNICAL EDITORS Traci Bunkers, Jean Lampe
ILLUSTRATIONS Lorrie LeJeune and Interweave Press
PHOTOGRAPHY Joe Coca
PHOTO STYLING Leigh Radford
COVER DESIGN Leigh Radford, Bren Frisch
INTERIOR DESIGN Leigh Radford
PRODUCTION Samantha L. Thaler
PROOFREADER AND INDEXER Nancy Arndt

Interweave Press, Inc.
201 East Fourth Street
Loveland, Colorado 80537-5655 USA
www.interweave.com

Printed in China by Midas

Library of Congress Cataloging-in-Publication Data

Galeskas, Beverly, 1950-
Felted knits / Beverly Galeskas.
p. cm.
ISBN 1-931499-33-0
1. Knitting--Patterns. 2. Felting. I. Title.
TT820.G15 2003
746.43'204--dc21
2003011109

10 9 8 7 6 5

acknowledgments

I cannot begin to thank all the people who helped with this book without first thanking my family: To my husband Joe, who not only worked hard to keep Fiber Trends running, but who also cooked for me and reminded me to sleep once in a while. I could not have done this book without him. To my son Scott and his wife Pam, who spent many weekends helping out so I could work on projects for the book. And to my father, who couldn't be here to see this book, but who taught me from childhood to always go after what I wanted, and never to quit before a job was done.

A very special thank you to Debbie Radtke, my friend, proofreader, and test knitter. Believe me, there is nothing better than having a best friend who can save you from your own words when you need it. Karen Aho of Acorn Street Shop, another good friend, deserves a special thank you. She offered a steady supply of yarn and encouragement, which I seemed to need in equal amounts. And to Meg Swansen: Thank you for your words of wisdom and encouragement when I needed them the most.

Even though the good folks at Interweave Press were kind enough to put my name on the cover, we all know that a book is really the work of many talented people. A special thank you to my editor, Lorrie LeJeune, for her many long hours of hard work, her constant positive attitude, and her skill at putting my words in order. To all the staff at Interweave Press—especially Leigh Radford who used her artistic talents to pull everything together and make it look good—thank you!

Last but not least, here's to all of the knitters who are reading this book. Without you there would be no need for knitting books, so you deserve the biggest thanks of all.

CONTENTS the art of

shrinking your knitting

preface

The art of shrinking your knitting Like many knitters and nonknitters alike, I had anything but a happy experience the first time I felted. Shortly after learning to knit, I invested in a beautiful white lambswool and angora yarn and knitted a sweater I was very proud of. Being white, it soon needed washing, and this was when I learned about felting. No, I wasn't so naive as to throw the sweater in the washing machine, but I did do some vigorous scrubbing on the sleeves to get them clean. When the sweater was dry the sleeves were too short and rather stiff. Stretching brought back some of the length, but the sweater was never the same again.

Seeing into the future would have eased my sadness over the loss of my angora sweater. It was about fifteen years later that felting my knitting on purpose not only became my passion, but played a valuable role in my business. Since then, I have felted literally hundreds of items in dozens of different yarns. Many projects have been successful and some not so successful, but each has been a learning experience.

One of the first things I learned is that it takes at least twice as long to felt something on purpose as it does to felt it by accident. The second thing I learned is that this slowness is a good thing. Slow felting is much easier to control than fast felting. When you are felting something you have spent time and money making, control is very important.

My goal in this book is to share some of my felting experience. On the following pages you will find many hints and tips along with very specific instructions for what I call Controlled Felting. This method gives me the most consistent results, but it is by no means the only way to felt. If you want to, you can even felt something by throwing it in a mud puddle and stomping on it. This is not a recommended way to arrive at a perfectly shaped hat or pair of slippers, but it could be great for working off aggression.

Felted knits are ideal projects for beginning and experienced knitters alike. Beginners will find many easy-to-knit projects here and will come to appreciate the glitches that felting can hide. Slightly uneven gauge, that funny looking stitch, or even a small hole, literally disappear in the wash. Experienced knitters will most likely enjoy trying some of the more involved shapes and may want to take up the challenge of designing their own project. Everyone can enjoy experimenting with the many different yarns available today, each of which will create a unique fabric when felted.

PART ONE introduction

what is felting?

Felt has existed for thousands of years. It may have been the first fabric ever made, and was most likely discovered by accident. There are numerous fables and legends about when and how the first felt came about, but of course no one knows for sure. I think it would be safe to say that humans and animals did not share this planet long before it became obvious to the humans that an animal's hair helped to protect it from the elements. It was then only natural that humans would learn to use that hair to insulate themselves from those same elements. And not long after that, humans discovered that animal hair that was slept on or wrapped around their hands or feet turned into felt over time. You can experience this same process if you wear socks or mittens made from wool that is not superwash treated. Over time, body heat, perspiration, friction, and pressure all play a part in turning the wool into felted fabric.

FELTING OR FULLING?

At any gathering of fiber artists, if you mention that you are going to felt your knitting, someone is sure to correct you. They will explain that if you start with a knitted item you are fulling, not felting. *Felting* is traditionally defined as creating a fabric from wool batting or fleece. *Fulling* is traditionally defined as creating a fabric from a woven or knitted fabric. The term fulling comes from the early textile industry in Britain, although it probably also has Roman roots. An absorbent clay, mined from the earth, was used along with other substances to degrease, clean, and bleach woven cloth and tighten (full) the weave into a strong fabric. The clay became known as "fullers earth" and the tradesmen who did this work were called "fullers."

So are we felting or fulling? Maybe what we are doing does not fit either description exactly. One thing is certain: we are creating a felt fabric, and since we begin with knitting, the term "felted knitting" seems to fit.

Is there a difference between a felted knit and a shrunken knit? Not necessarily. Sometimes the difference is only in whether the felting was intentional or not. Most of the projects shown in this book are felted until the stitches disappear. This process creates a felt fabric look, as opposed to a shrunken knitting look.

HOW FELTING OCCURS

Animal hair, including human hair, is covered with scales. Under a powerful microscope a hair looks something like a rod covered with fish scales or the bark of a tree. The technical term for your hair's outer covering is the cuticle.

Moisture and heat cause these scales to soften and rise slightly from the hair shaft. If they are then exposed to friction or pressure while in this softened state, they begin to lock together. The more friction, the tighter they lock, and eventually the individual hairs become a thick, matted (felt) fabric. If you apply this treatment to your own hair you will have dreadlocks. Felting is not a reversible process. You can stretch a felt fabric to make it larger, but you cannot unfelt it.

The most important things you need to know about felted knits:

- Felting is an art, not a science.
- Every item will be unique, and each time you felt, you will learn something new.
- Make samples! For satisfactory results you must know how your yarn will felt.
- Controlling the felting process is the only way to control the finished size.

felting basics

The two Icelandic yarns shown under the purses on the opposite page appear very similar. The two purses made from these wools, however, are very different. Both were knit on the same size needles with the same number of stitches, and they were the same size before felting. They both felted easily, and resulted in attractive, though very different fabrics. The most surprising result was the difference in size and proportion. Why did this happen? The purse on the top was made out of Reynolds Lopi, a single-ply Icelandic yarn spun in Iceland. The purse on the bottom was made out of Tongue River Farm's single-ply Icelandic yarn, which is grown and spun in the USA. Both yarns are made out of wool from Icelandic sheep, but the Tongue River Farm flock is sheared more frequently, and the fleece processed differently than fleece spun in Iceland. The result is two yarns that look very similar, but felt very differently. This illustrates why it is so important to test-felt your yarn before starting a project.

GETTING STARTED

One of the most frequently asked questions from knitters new to felting is, Do I have to use 100% wool? The answer is that 100% wool is usually a good choice for felting, but other animal fibers such as alpaca, mohair, angora, and llama also work. Some of these fibers felt well on their own, and some are best used along with sheep's wool. A yarn may also have a certain percentage of synthetic, say 15% nylon, and still felt successfully. The felting ability of a fiber blend depends on the characteristics of the wool part and the number of wool fibers that can interact with one another. You can even use a strand of 100% synthetic yarn if you knit it with a strand of strong felting wool. This process appears in several projects in this book.

Another common question is, If I match the unfelted gauge stated in my pattern, won't the felted size also match? Not necessarily. Every yarn reacts differently when felted. Sometimes even different colors of the same yarn felt to a different gauge or texture of fabric. This feature is why just matching the unfelted gauge of a pattern in no way guarantees that you will get the desired results. The purses on page 4 illustrate a few of these differences.

The last most common question asked by knitters new to felting is, How much bigger do I knit something if I want to felt it? You'll find the answer to that question a little later in the section on designing your own felted knits.

CHOOSING YARNS FOR A FELTED KNIT PROJECT

If you are following a pattern in this book, or another felted knitting pattern and you use the same yarn in the same color as shown, you can safely skip the testing process. Otherwise you have no way of assuring your success without taking the following steps.

First, consider the color. While there is no way to say for sure which colors of a particular yarn will felt and to what degree, my experience provides some general guidelines.

- Bleached white will not felt. This is most likely due to damage done by the bleach to the scales of the fiber cuticle. Avoid any yarn that looks bright white.
- Light, clear colors may also be resistant to felting. This also may be due to a bleaching process prior to dyeing.
- Natural white and ecru will often felt poorly, although there are a few natural white yarns on the market that felt beautifully. You should not assume however, that if you can successfully felt Brand X yarn in navy that Brand X natural white will felt successfully as well. As with bleached yarns, many natural whites receive some type of processing to lighten and even out the color.
- Heather shades—those with natural, undyed fibers spun in—usually result in a very nice fabric, but they often felt more slowly than solid-dyed colors. It's always a good idea to run a careful test before you use a heathered yarn and a solid for different areas of the same item.

Read your yarn label

It's a good idea to check the yarn's suggested gauge, but do not match it to your pattern's suggested gauge. Felted knitting projects are almost always knitted at a very loose gauge, using a needle at least 2 to 3 sizes larger than what you would use if you were knitting a garment in the same yarn. However, the label's gauge information is a useful guideline for determining whether the yarn is of an appropriate weight for your project. Don't put too much emphasis on an exact match. Recommended gauges vary considerably from manufacturer to manufacturer, even though the yarn is of similar weight.

AVOID SUPERWASH WOOL

The superwash mark, or any reference to machine washability on the label, means that the yarn has been treated to *prevent* it from felting. Obviously you won't want to use it for a felted knitting project! Unfortunately, wools sometimes receive this treatment but are not labeled as machine washable. The only way to determine suitability for sure is by test-felting a sample.

Where did the wool come from?

A fact you may not be aware of is that wool varies from breed to breed and even from sheep to sheep. Information about the fiber's origin is not often included on the label, which is another reason test-felting is always necessary. If you are using your own handspun yarn, or any wool from a sheep you know, you can check a good fiber reference book such as *In Sheep's Clothing: A Handspinner's Guide to Wool* (Interweave Press, 2003) to learn about its felting qualities. However, nothing is better than a test swatch or small project to learn about the felting characteristics of any yarn, commercial or handspun.

TEST-FELTING YOUR YARN

While it's not a substitute for an actual knitted test sample, you can run a quick felting test to determine whether to proceed with your yarn choice. Break off about a yard of your yarn and wet it with warm water. Add a drop of dishwashing liquid and roll it around between your hands as if you were making a little ball of cookie dough. After a few minutes, examine the sample closely. If it has felted into a firm ball, then your yarn is more than likely a good choice for felting, and you now know it is worth the time to make a test swatch. If the ball is not really firm, try to pull it apart and see what happens. Even some superwash yarns mat together and appear to ball up, but on close examination they pull apart into a mess of fuzz. These yarns are not good choices for felting.

THE ACTUAL TEST SAMPLE

If you intend to make something small, such as baby booties or a small purse, then you may choose to just forge ahead, since these items are really no larger than a test swatch. You'll be experimenting, so be prepared for anything. For a large project you will not want to skip the test-felting. Even for something like a tote bag, where finished size is not critical, it's still worthwhile to see what the yarn will look like when it is felted. That way you'll know if you want to invest your time working with it. If you hate knitting swatches, then make a small project instead. One of the smaller bags on page 23 or 25 would make a good project for testing yarns. They have the advantage of being usable, even if your yarn does not felt in the way that you had hoped.

If your project includes areas of different yarns or colors, then use all of them in your sample. You need to know whether they will felt to the same size, and at the same rate. If yarn A and yarn B both felt to a beautiful fabric, but yarn A felts in 10 minutes and yarn B needs 45 minutes of agitation to achieve the same look, they are not compatible for use in the same piece.

Thread markers to check gauge

After knitting your swatch or trial project, be sure to take notes and insert thread markers before felting. For example: Use cotton thread to mark off 18 sts and 18 rows in the center of your sample. Be sure to write down how many stitches and rows are between your thread markers. If gauge is critical to your project, you may want to make a larger sample and mark off more stitches and rows.

Felt your swatch or sample project, using the same method you plan to use for your project, and allow it to air dry. If you don't like the look of the result, then you will want to choose a different yarn and start the testing process over.

If your sample looks good, measure and calculate the number of stitches and rows to the inch and determine your felted gauge. Here's an example of how it's done. If you marked off 18 sts and that section measures 3 inches after felting, divide 18 by 3 to arrive at a gauge of 6 sts to an inch. Do the same for the row gauge. Check these numbers against your pattern. If your sample matches the pattern, you can begin knitting with confidence. If it's not an exact match, but is less than a quarter of a stitch per inch off, you can probably still use the yarn and felt the project to the correct size. Remember that you will be controlling the felting process and can stop it when the size is right.

Sometimes your test piece will produce a beautiful fabric, but at a gauge that is very different from your pattern. In this case you will either need to calculate changes to the pattern's stitch and row count or use the yarn in a different pattern.

PREPARING A PROJECT FOR FELTING

Seams

In felted knits, you usually want your seams to disappear in the fabric. To achieve this effect you want flat, loose seams that are about the same thickness as your knitting. Always use your project yarn to sew seams. A good method for joining your pieces is a loose, overcast stitch worked from the right side (wrong sides together). If you use a sharp needle and just catch the edges together, the seam will lie flat when opened out.

Working in ends

Loose ends need to be carefully secured, but never in a way that causes extra bulk. Thread the loose end through a sharp needle. Then, working on the wrong side, skim though the backs of the stitches in one direction for at least an inch. Work back in the other direction for another inch, skimming along the side of, rather than the top of, your first pass of stitching. After working in all the ends, stretch the fabric gently in all directions. Trim the remainder of each yarn end close to the fabric. If you are working with a slippery novelty yarn, leave an inch or so of tail until after felting. This will help keep the ends from popping out during the felting process. Trim the ends close to the fabric when the project is complete.

Holes in your knitting

Murphy has a law about holes when it comes to felting: If you make holes on purpose, such as eyelets for a lacing or a drawstring, they will completely disappear during felting. If, on the other hand, you leave an accidental hole, it will remain a hole no matter how tightly you felt the fabric!

To overcome Murphy's Law of Holes, check your knitting over carefully before felting. If you find an unintentional hole, be sure to mend it. Use your sharp needle and a length of your project yarn to darn it closed. Use only enough stitches and yarn to close the hole; do not create a thick area.

To make sure any eyelets or buttonholes remain open after felting, thread a length of thick cotton yarn through them and tie the ends securely. Cotton yarn does not stick to wool and will easily pull out after your item is felted.

Swatches

Swatches clockwise: Sample A shows two yarns that have felted at the same rate. They are compatible and a good choice for combining in the same project.

Sample B shows two yarns that both felt well, but not at the same rate. The yarn on the bottom has felted faster than the yarn on the top. These yarns should not be combined in the same project.

Sample C shows that adding a nonfelting novelty yarn to wool will sometimes result in only a slight difference in gauge.

Sample D shows that sometimes adding a novelty yarn results in a more drastic change in gauge.

Always test a novelty yarn combination ahead of time so you can adjust your stitch count to allow for any gauge change.

A
B
C
D

CONTROLLED FELTING IN THE WASHING MACHINE

There are many ways to felt a piece of knitting, and you will find a wide variety of instructions in patterns for felted knits. The following method comes from my experience of felting hundreds of items—some successfully and some not. This method may not be the fastest one, but it allows you to get just the size you want. (Note that these are general directions. Some projects in this book have special needs and require that you follow additional steps or instructions. Remember to always check your pattern for specific information before proceeding.)

The felting process can take anywhere from ten minutes to over an hour. If you're interrupted or need to take a break, just turn your washing machine off. It will not harm your project to leave it soaking for a while. If you return to find that your water has cooled, you may want add more hot water.

Step One Place your knitting in a zippered pillow protector, or at the very least, a fine mesh bag. The mesh bag is adequate for most wool, but a pillow protector gives better protection if you are felting with Icelandic-type wool, mohair, or any other hairy fiber. Modern washers are not designed to handle the amount of fiber that is washed out during felting. Most machines cycle water through the pump during agitation. Over time the loose fibers accumulate in the workings of the pump until it begins to leak. This problem is easily avoided by using a bag, so please don't let the fear of damaging your washing machine keep you away from felting.

Step Two Set the water temperature of your washer to hot. Standard hot-water tank temperature is sufficient. Adding boiling water does not speed felting time and can result in painful burns. Hot water helps to soften the fibers and raise the scales of the cuticle, but it is agitation, or movement, that causes the friction between the fibers and accomplishes the actual work of felting. To achieve enough agitation for successful felting, you need a relatively small amount of water and strong agitation. So set your washer for a small load, and moderate to high agitation. Experience (and lots of test swatches) will determine the best settings for your washer and the type of fiber you're felting.

Step Three Add a small amount of a mild detergent—or better yet, a rinse-free wool wash such as Woolmix or Eucalan (available at many yarn shops or by mail order. See list of suppliers on page 109). The detergent or wool wash combined with the hot water will further soften the fibers and prepare them for felting. The obvious advantage to using a rinse-free product is that you can skip the rinsing step. If you do choose to use detergent, employ a mild one without added bleach or fabric softeners. A clear, mild dishwashing liquid works well and may be easier to rinse out than some laundry detergents.

How much washing agent do you need? For a small item or two, a tablespoon or less is sufficient. You want to use enough to help with the softening process, but too much can actually hinder the felting by coating the fibers. If your water feels slippery and you have mounds

LET YOUR WASHER DO THE WORK WHILE YOU STAY IN CONTROL!

of suds, that is too much. Drain some sudsy water and add more water to dilute the soap.

Step Four If needed, add a larger object to increase the agitation. Agitation is necessary for felting to occur, and one or two small items in a washer by themselves will only bob around gently. Unless you are felting a large project, adding something heavy like an old pair of jeans will greatly increase the agitation and speed up the felting process. Other safe items to add include tennis balls, rubber flip-flop thongs, or any fairly heavy piece of old clothing that will not shed. It's important not to add something that will shed lint into the water, because it will become part of your felt. Many felting projects have been decorated with flecks of terrycloth from old bath towels. (Even old towels can lose a fair amount of lint in each wash.) Adding a load of the family laundry to your felting bath is not a good idea, either. The amount of agitation needed to felt something is usually far more than what is needed to clean your clothing and will only subject the garments to extra wear.

Step Five Start your washer and set your timer. Check the progress of your item every 5 to 10 minutes at the beginning, and more frequently as your project nears the desired size. Keep resetting your washer to continue agitating as long as necessary. *Do not let it drain and spin!*

This agitation period is the "controlled" part of the felting method. You have to regularly fish your project out of the washer, squeeze the water out, and see how it's doing. Depending on your wool, your water, your machine, the phase of the moon, and any number of other factors, it may take anywhere from a few minutes to an hour to get the results you want. By checking frequently you can stop the process at just the right time. If you are felting more than one item at a time, be sure to check all of them. Each item needs to be taken out of its bag, examined, shaped and admired, then returned for more agitation as needed.

When your project appears to be the perfect size, remove it from the washer. *Do not leave it in to spin and rinse.* The spin cycle may set permanent creases in your felt and machine rinsing will cause further shrinkage. Remember, there is no magic predetermined stopping point for felting, so you have to stop the process when you have what you want.

Step Six Rinsing. You can skip this step if you use a rinse-free wool wash such as Woolmix or Eucalan. If you need to rinse, do it by hand in cool to warm water. Holding a felted object under very cold, running water will sometimes help firm up the felt—if that's what you desire. Otherwise, rinse the object in lukewarm water. Either way, be sure to rinse until all traces of soap are removed.

There are many ways to felt. If you get results that you are happy with by using methods other than this one, by all means use them. On the other hand, if your pattern recommends a method that sounds risky to you, such as putting your project through the washer and dryer with a load of laundry, don't hesitate to substitute a more controlled method.

CONTROLLED FELTING IN THE WASHING MACHINE

FELTING LARGE PROJECTS

As a general rule, the larger the item, the faster it will felt. When you're dealing with something as large as a vest, be very careful not to over-felt it. To slow down the process use your washer's highest water level and the delicate cycle. Do a progress check every 5 minutes.

GETTING TO KNOW YOUR WASHING MACHINE

Experiment with your washer to see how the water level and cycle affect the amount of agitation. Each brand of washer has its own characteristics, but in general, for vigorous agitation, use a low water level and a regular or heavy-duty cycle. For gentle agitation use a full water level and a delicate or woolen cycle.

FELTING IN A FRONT-LOADING WASHING MACHINE

It is possible to felt in some front-loading washers. A few of these machines are designed so that the water level falls below the door when the machine is stopped. If you have this type of machine, you can follow the felting instructions on this page, stopping and checking your progress as needed. You will most likely have to wait a minute or two after stopping the machine before you can open the door.

Other front-loading machines are designed with a door that remains locked until the cycle is complete. Controlled felting in these machines is impossible. If you have this type of washer, you may want to entice a friend who owns a top-loading machine with a pair of felted slippers in return for the use of the top-loader. Your other option is to go ahead and use the full cycle on your front-loading machine, but this option is not recommended.

FELTING BY HAND

Hand felting can be a quick and fun way to felt a small project. Larger projects, or those like slippers, that need to be felted to an extra firm fabric are usually best done in a washing machine.

If you intend to felt your items by hand, prepare them the same way you would for machine felting. Refer to page 8 for tips on working in ends and sewing any seams.

To felt by hand pour a few inches of hot, but not boiling, water in the tub, and add a teaspoon or two of detergent or wool wash. Place your project in the hot soapy water and begin kneading and rubbing, much as you would knead bread dough. (You can wear rubber gloves to keep your hands from chapping.) Constantly change the direction you work to insure even felting. At first it may seem as if nothing will ever happen, but be patient and keep rubbing and kneading. Suddenly, you will feel the wool start to felt. It's just like magic!

Once felting begins, pay special attention to molding and shaping to get the look you want. You are in charge of deciding when your project is felted to perfection, but don't give in to the temptation to stop too soon. If things seem to be happening too slowly, you may want to give your project a dip into cold water from time to time, squeeze it out, then plunge it back into hot water. Alternating between hot and cold water shocks the fibers and sometimes speeds the felting process along.

If you have used a rinse-free wool wash, you may skip the rinsing step. If you used detergent, soap, or shampoo, rinse well, and be sure that you remove all traces of soap. Block and finish your item as described on page 14 or in the pattern.

For hand felting you need:

1. A sink or tub that holds several inches of hot water.
2. Woolmix, Eucalan, or another rinse-free wool wash; soap or detergent.
3. Several towels.
4. A second sink or tub of cold water. (Helpful, but not required.)
5. Enough time. Hand felting can take a while.

THE FINISHING TOUCHES: BLOCKING, DRYING, AND GROOMING

Blocking

Always refer to your pattern for any special blocking instructions, but no matter what you are making, the time to get it into the shape you want is *immediately* after the final rinse. Wet felt is very pliable and can be stretched, pulled, pushed, or stuffed until it looks exactly right. Here's what to do.

First roll your item in towels and squeeze to remove as much water as possible. After towel drying, a small, flat item, such as an evening bag, usually needs only a slight shaping to straighten the sides. It can then be dried flat.

A hat looks best if you stretch it over a hat form, a head-sized bowl, or a ball. Then you can hand-shape the brim to the desired look. The hat should remain on the form until it is completely dry, although it is fine to remove it periodically to try on and admire.

Mittens and slippers are best shaped on your hands or feet—or someone else's if you can find a willing helper of the right size. You can stuff slippers with fiberfill (polyester stuffing) if needed to hold the shape until dry. Set mittens on a towel to dry, taking care to maintain the curved hand shape. (Other three-dimensional shapes such as toys and pillows may also benefit from being stuffed with fiberfill while wet.)

For a garment such as a vest, use a tape measure to make sure that both the length and width are correct. If necessary, you can stretch the wet felt to gain another inch or so in one direction or the other. Make sure that the front edges are the same length, and that the bottom edge is straight and even.

No matter what you are making, do not leave it to dry until you are completely happy with its size and how it looks.

DRYING AND GROOMING

Drying a felted item in your clothes dryer will undo all the effort you put into getting the size and shape just right. Instead, be patient and air dry the item away from sunlight. In the winter you may place your felted item near, but not on, a forced air register to take advantage of the warm dry air.

Once your project is dry, clip any loose ends and do any other necessary grooming. Some fibers look best if they are brushed, while others may even be trimmed or sheared to get the look you want.

CARING FOR YOUR FELTED KNITS

Felted knitting is very durable and quite water-resistant. A light brushing with a bristle clothes brush from time to time will remove surface soil, but eventually most items will need to be washed. Do not use the machine for washing unless you want more shrinkage. Instead, hand wash the item as you would a wool sweater, then block and dry it the same way you did after felting.

Sometimes after only a little use, you will find that your slippers, tote bag, or hat have stretched out and are really too big. In this case you will want to use the washer to shrink the item more. First soak it in hot water until it is thoroughly wet, then use the controlled felting method to bring it down to the desired size. Watch it very closely because this second felting may need only a short agitation time.

DESIGNING YOUR OWN PROJECT

Now that you understand the process of felting, you can start designing your own felted knits. The first question most knitters ask is, How much bigger do you knit your item in order to get the right felted size? Many people hope that determining a percentage of shrinkage will allow them to calculate the finished size, but unfortunately that doesn't always work. The answer to the question is there is no answer.

We have already discovered that each yarn felts differently. When you're designing for felting, you also have to deal with how the shape of the item changes the felted gauge. This process is most easily illustrated by the examples on page 16.

Note the drastic difference between the size and shape of Sample 1 and the size and shape of the same number of stitches and rows in Sample 2. This difference is caused by the weight of the two ends stretching the center of this long narrow piece during the felting process.

Sample 1 is the type of swatch you will most likely use to determine the felted gauge of a particular yarn. It's fairly accurate when used to plan a hat, tote bag, or vest. Sample 2 is a useful sample only if you are making something long and thin, but it does show us the effect of shape on felted gauge. This difference in gauge will show up in such things as a narrow bag or cell-phone holder, the front of an open vest above the armhole, the legs and arms on a felt toy, or any piece that is much longer than it is wide. Expect the same type of results when the width greatly exceeds the length of a piece.

These samples reveal another interesting bit of information. The total measurements are larger than the gauge would indicate. This discrepancy is due to the fact that the center of a piece always felts more than the edges; it's also why the edges of the samples are distorted. Without some preplanning, this discrepancy presents a problem in many designs.

The vest on page 62 uses two different methods of controlling this problem. The fronts and armholes have a border that is knit on after felting. To stabilize the fronts and armholes during felting and control their length, a cotton border was knit on before felting. Without this border, the edges of the felted vest would resemble the edges of these samples. The bottom edge needed a different treatment, because it has no added border. To keep it from flaring during felting, about 20% fewer stitches than needed for each size were cast on. Several rows were worked on this reduced stitch count before increasing to the number needed for the vest body. This is a very easy way to control a cast-on or cast-off edge. The edges of smaller items such as purses can usually be kept straight with only a 10% to 15% difference in stitch count.

With these examples in mind, think about the shape of the item you want to create. You can use this knowledge, along with your felted gauge sample, to make your first estimate of how large your project should be. Then you will need to knit and felt it to see how close your estimates were. Before you felt, make some careful notes about stitch and row counts and mark several areas to measure for gauge. Felting is not an exact science, so be prepared to knit your samples several times before you get the results you want. The knowledge you gain from doing samples will be well rewarded with beautiful felted knits.

WHEN THINGS GO WRONG

Common Felting Problems

Taking the time to do your test felting and making those early progress checks in the washing machine can prevent most felting disasters. (Remember that your test piece can be a small project, not just a swatch.) But even with the most careful planning and attention to detail, problems occasionally do occur.

The most common problem you'll encounter is slow felting. It's rarely a serious problem, and in most cases, the solution is to adjust your process or your expectations. First, check that you are getting strong agitation. If not, put a pair or two of jeans in with your item and try again.

Adding a larger, heavier item to the washer increases agitation and often solves the problem. Time is the other factor. Some yarns just take longer to felt than others, no matter what you do. Most of the tips and tricks for speeding up felting are no more than whatever someone tried at the time the yarn was finally ready to felt. My favorite trick is to leave the item to soak overnight. I tell myself that it is the fear of drowning that encourages yarn to felt. More likely, an extended soaking softens resistant fibers and makes them more capable of felting.

Another common problem is combining yarns or colors that felt very differently. (Remember that similar yarns can react very differently to felting. See samples on page 4.) Fortunately, this problem becomes apparent during test felting so you can easily avoid it in a large project. The felting characteristics of yarn are not something you can change, so if you're not happy with your finished fabric, you'll need to try again with another yarn or another combination.

If you combine colors in your felted knits, you're also likely to encounter fiber migration. Migration happens when dark fibers released during agitation become felted into the light sections of your item and alter its color. The reverse also happens (light fibers felted into dark areas), but light to dark migration is usually much less noticeable. There is no cure for fiber migration, so choose your color combinations knowing migration may happen. Dye migration can also change color, but it is far less common. If dye migrates in a test project, try lowering the water temperature.

Both these samples were knit in worsted-weight yarn on a size 10½ needle, then felted in a washing machine for the same length of time.

(Sample A) There are 30 sts and 50 rows on this sample and it measured 8" x 10.5" (20.5 x 26.5 cm) before felting. After felting, it measures 6.75" wide x 5" (17 x 12.5 cm) long, and has a gauge at the center of 4 sts and 8 rows to an inch. This sample illustrates the fact that in a square piece, stockinette stitch shrinks more in length than in width.

(Sample B) This sample is knitted in the same yarn at the same gauge and is also 30 sts wide, but has 90 rows. It measured 8" x 19" (20.5 x 48.5 cm) before felting. The section marked in cotton at the center has the same number of stitches and rows as Sample A. This area measures 5" wide x 6" (12.5 x 15 cm) long. The gauge at the center is 5.7 sts and 6.66 rows to an inch.

Problems in the Washing Machine

Occasionally during the agitation phase, parts of your project may stick together. Don't panic. Gently pull the pieces apart, reshape the item, then return it to the washer for a few more minutes of felting. Repeat the process as needed, and keep a close watch on the item. Once the fabric begins to firm up, the tendency for parts to felt together is reduced.

When you're machine felting, especially in the early stages, your project will be very stretchy. The weight of the wet wool may distort the piece. Mittens are a good example. If left unattended during felting, they can become too long and narrow. The solution to stretching is the same as above: Pull the item back into the shape you want and return it to the washer for a few more minutes of felting. Repeat the reshaping as often as necessary.

Having a piece stick together or stretch shows why it is so important to monitor the felting process. Take your item out of the washer frequently to examine it. It's much easier to correct problems during felting than afterward.

When True Disaster Strikes

What do you do when you seem to have a real disaster in the making? Maybe you skimped a little during the testing process and now have a pair of slippers with nearly felted soles and tops, but cuffs that are way behind and look as though they may not felt until next spring. You can salvage such a project with a little work. Stop the felting process as soon as you see that the fabric is uneven. Remove the item from the washer and roll it in towels to remove some of the water. Using a piece of elastic cord and a large, sharp needle, thread the elastic into the cuff so it won't show. Pull the piece up to the right size, tie the elastic securely, then bury the ends inside the cuff. Return the slippers to the washer to finish felting. The elastic can be left in to help keep the cuffs from stretching during normal wear.

Elastic works well for cuffs and other edges, but what if a whole area of your item is not felting? For example, the soles and cuffs of your slippers are felting fine, but the main upper sections are not. Stop the felting process as soon as the problem becomes apparent. First, try hand felting on the stubborn area. Sometimes that helps it catch up with the rest of the item. If hand felting doesn't work, find a length of lightweight wool that you know will felt quickly and easily. (It's great if the color matches your item, but it's not critical.) Using a sharp needle, work the lightweight wool into the slipper wool on the wrong side, making sure that it doesn't show on the right side. Sew several rows of stitches in both directions to form a loose mesh of new wool. Secure the ends and begin felting again. Keep a close eye on what is happening. If all goes well, the new wool will shrink quickly and pull the slipper fiber in with it.

Perhaps your felting is going too fast rather than too slow. You may have waited too long between progress checks and now your item is smaller than you wanted it to be. Very often you can fix this problem just by stretching the wet wool to the right size. (You may need an extra pair of hands to help with such stretching.) Once stretched, the item must remain at the proper size until dry. Stretching a hat over a bowl or a hat form will do the trick. Other items can be pinned out to size or stuffed with something to hold their shape. Of course, there are limits to how much an item can be stretched. If it's really too small no matter what you do, you need to take a deep breath and make a new one.

Turning Lemons into Lemonade

Sooner or later you will have a true felting disaster. It happens to all of us. If you're interested in experimenting with new yarns and shapes, disasters are unavoidable. And while they're disappointing, disasters are actually opportunities for learning. Take a close look at your item. It may not be what you wanted, but it may spark an idea for a whole new project. The little dresser tray on page 89 is a good example of lemonade made from a lemon. While experimenting with coasters and trivets, I tried putting an I-cord border on a diagonally knit trivet. The I-cord edges felted much too tight and turned what should have been a flat piece into a small bowl. I might never have figured out how to do this if it hadn't happened by accident!

Sometimes there is nothing to do but laugh at your results and, of course, learn something new about felting. I will admit to having a rather large stash of "learning pieces." What can you do with them? Before tossing something in the trash, consider cutting and resewing it into a new shape or making appliqués out of it. If it looks really interesting, hang it on the wall and call it experimental art.

PART TWO
projects

you can take it with you

Simple bags and purses are great projects for first-time felters, or for testing new yarns for the first time. Size often doesn't matter, so your finished project is useful even if your yarn does not felt as you expect it to. It is fun to experiment with combinations of wool and novelty yarns for unique felted purses and totes.

bags

SMALL AND EASY PURSES

Small purses are so easy to make that you can have one for every mood! They're also great for trying out new yarns and color combinations. When you're experimenting with different yarn weights, choose a needle several sizes larger than your yarn would normally need. Aim for a loose gauge that will allow the yarns to felt to a nice fabric.

STRAPS

Felted I-cord straps work on as few as 2 sts for a thin cord, to as many as 7 sts for a thick cord. It may be sewn to the bag either before or after felting. If you are unsure of the length you want, felt the strap separately, then cut to size before attaching it to the bag.

When felted, most I-cord will lose only about 15% of its knitted length. It may appear slightly shorter at first, but it will stretch with use. For instructions on knitting I-cord, see Techniques, page 103.

If you prefer to add a **nonfelted strap** when your purse is complete, consider using twisted cord or braid made with either matching or contrasting yarn. Leather, webbing, or chain are also good choices.

When sewing on straps before felting, be sure to use the same wool that the purse or strap is made in. The stitches will felt right along with the purse. To attach straps or chain after felting, use a strong thread such as buttonhole or carpet thread in a matching color. If the stitches are on the outside of your bag and the thread is not a good color match, cover it with a stitch or two of the matching wool.

CLOSURES

Buttons, snaps, or other fasteners should be sewn on after your project is felted and dry. For added strength use a heavy-duty sewing thread. Buttonholes may be cut in the finished felt, but they should be overstitched to keep them from stretching and fraying. An easier solution is to make button loops. These can be made in purchased cording, elastic cord, leather, or twisted cord. Cut a 4 to 6 inch length, fold in half and knot ends, adjusting the size of the loop to fit your button. Sew on with heavy-duty thread after your item is felted and dry. If your button loop is sewn to the right side, you may want to cover the sewing thread with a few stitches of wool to match your bag or add a second button to cover the stitching.

Gift Bags

The quickest and easiest of projects, these little bags are my first choice for test-felting yarns or using up small amounts of leftover yarn. Use them as decorative ornaments at the holidays, or place small gifts inside for special people!

With circular needle in the appropriate size for your yarn, cast on 30 (44) sts. Place marker and join, being careful not to twist sts. Work in rounds of St st (knit every rnd) for 22 (32) rnds.

Note: If your cast-on edge is too tight to allow the sts to be joined in the round, try using a larger needle to cast on and work very loosely.

Garter-Stitch Border

Purl 1 rnd, knit 1 rnd, purl 1 rnd. Bind off all sts knitwise.

Finishing

Sew cast-on edge together for bottom seam. Weave in loose ends on WS. When the bag is felted and dry, sew or tie on a short length of twisted cord or ribbon for the handle.

SIZE

The size of the finished bag will vary depending on the yarn and the number of stitches used. Two stitch counts are given, but any even number may be used. The bags shown measure about 4½" (11.5 cm) square.

YARN

About 55 yards (50 meters) of worsted-weight for a 44-st bag or 40 yards (36.5 meters) of bulky-weight for a 30-st bag. Using other st counts will require more or less yardage. The three gift bags shown on the left were knit on a size 11 (8 mm) circular needle at 30 sts in Baabajoes 14-ply Woolpak (bulky) (100% wool; 310 yd [283.5 m]/250 g): #35 aubergine; #27 goldstone; #8 plum, 1 skein for each bag. For the worsted-weight yarn (not shown here) we used Mountain Colors Mountain Goat (55%, 45% wool; 240 yd [219.5 m] 4 oz), 1 skein.

NEEDLES

Choose a needle several sizes larger than your yarn would normally require. For bulky: Size 11 or 13 (8 or 9 mm), 16"(40 cm) circular. For worsted: Size 10 or 10½ (6 or 6.5 mm), 16" (40 cm) circular.

NOTIONS

Marker; tapestry needle; desired length of twisted cord or ribbon for handle.

GAUGE

Gauge will vary with yarn used and is not critical for these patterns. If you are testing a yarn for another project, be sure to note the needle size you use and mark off sts to measure the felted gauge.

FELTING

Follow basic felting instructions on *page 10* *until bag is desired size.*

Small Purse

This bag is just big enough to hold your cell phone, lip-gloss, and credit card. The addition of a flap and button closure lends style and security.

Follow instructions for the Gift Bag, except complete 32 (42) rnds in St st (knit every rnd) before working the garter-stitch border.

Finishing

Sew cast-on edge together. Weave in loose ends on WS. Choose a strap style and decide whether you will add it before or after felting. (Purse is shown with a twisted cord strap made with 3 strands of worsted-weight wool that was sewn to the inside of the bag after it was felted and dry.)

Small Purse with Flap

With circular needle cast on 30 (44) sts. Place marker and join, being careful not to twist sts. Work in rounds of St st (knit every rnd) for 42 (52) rnds.
Dec rnd: K3, [k2tog, k5] 1 (2) times, k2tog, k18 (25)—28 (41) sts remain.
Next rnd: P13 (19), k15 (22).
Next rnd: Bind off 13 (19) sts, knit to end of rnd—15 (22) sts remain.

Flap

(Worked back and forth in rows.)
Row 1: (WS) K2, purl to last 2 sts, k2.
Row 2: Knit.
Repeat Rows 1 and 2 five (seven) more times, then repeat Row 1 once more.
Dec row: (RS) K3, [k2tog, k5] 1 (2) times, k2tog, k3—13 (19) sts.
Knit 2 rows of garter stitch. Bind off all sts, knitwise.

Strap

With dpn, cast on 3 sts and work in I-cord (see Techniques, page 103) for about 50" (127 cm). Cut yarn and draw tail through sts. Pull together tightly and fasten off.

Finishing

Sew cast-on edge together. Pin strap ends to each side of bag on the outside, beginning about 2½" (6.5 cm) down from the top edge. Slip-stitch into place. Weave in loose ends on WS. After felting, sew button to front of purse. Make button loop (see Closures, page 21) of elastic cord and sew to underside of flap.

SIZE

Finished size in yarns shown: 3½" by 6½" (9 by 16.5 cm).

YARN

***Small Purse:** 50 to 75 yards (46 to 68.5 meters) of worsted-weight (used single, or double to approximate bulky-weight) or bulky-weight yarn. The small purse shown was knit on a size 11 (8 mm) circular needle at 30 st, and took about 50 yd (46 m) each of Brown Sheep Nature Spun Worsted (100% wool; 245 yd [224 m]/100 g): #N62 amethyst, 1 skein; and Green Mountain Spinnery Mountain Mohair (70% wool, 30% mohair; 140 yd [128 m]/50 g): # 5 blue violet, 1 skein. Yarns were held together throughout. **Small Purse with flap:** 60 to 90 yards (55 to 82 m) depending on st count and yarn weight. The purse shown was knit on a size 11 (8 mm), 16" (40 cm) circular needle at 30 sts, and took about 75 yards (69 m) of Classic Elite Montera (50% llama/50% wool; 127 yd [117 m]/100 g): #3842 wine, 1 skein.*

NEEDLES

***Small Purse:** For bulky: Size 11 or 13 (8 or 9 mm), 16" (40 cm) circular and 2 double-pointed (dpn) for straps. For worsted: Size 10 or 10½ (6 or 6.5 mm), 16" (40 cm) circular and 2 dpn for straps. **Small Purse with flap:** Size 11 (8 mm), 16" (40 cm) circular and 2 dpn for straps.*

GAUGE

Gauge will vary with yarn used and is not critical for these patterns.

NOTIONS

Marker; tapestry needle; button loop (if desired).

Basic Everyday Purse

Extra easy to knit, these purses are really just enlarged versions of the gift bag and small purses on the previous pages. Instructions are written for the samples pictured, but you may adjust the yarn weight or stitch counts for a larger or smaller bag. If you choose a different weight of yarn, adjust your needle size accordingly by choosing several sizes larger than you would ordinarily use for the yarn. The basic everyday purse is big enough for daily use. For an interesting look, use two different color yarns held together.

Body

With circular needle and 1 strand each of colors A and B held together, cast on 50 sts. Place marker and join, being careful not to twist sts. Work in rounds of St st (knit every rnd) for about 42 rnds.

Garter-Stitch Border

Cut color B and add a 2nd strand of color A.
Rnd 1: Knit.
Rnd 2: Purl.
Repeat Rounds 1 and 2 once more. Bind off all sts knitwise.

With dpn and 2 strands of color A held together, cast on 5 sts and work in I-cord (see Techniques, page 103) for about 45" (114.5 cm). Cut yarn and draw tail through sts. Pull together tightly and fasten off.

Finishing

Sew cast-on edge together to close the bottom of the bag. Sew I-cord to side edges of bag, either on the inside or the outside, beginning 1" to 2" (2.5 to 5 cm) down from the top. Weave in loose ends on WS.

SIZE

Basic Everday Purse: *Finished size in yarns shown: 9" by 9½"(23 by 24 cm).* ***Basic Everyday Purse with flap:*** *Finished size in the yarn shown: 9" by 8" (23 by 20.5 cm).*

YARN

Basic Everyday Purse: *180 yards (164.5 meters) DK or worsted-weight (color A) and 110 yards (100.5 meters) bulky-weight (color B). The purse shown is made in Dale of Norway Heilo (color A) (100% wool; 108 yd [100 m]/50 g): color 83, charcoal, 2 skeins, and Ara (color B), (100% wool; 55 yd [50 m]/50 g): color 6, 2 skeins. (Note: the purse is shown here in a DK and a bulky-weight, but other weights may be substituted.)* ***Basic Everyday Purse with flap:*** *300 yards (274 m) of worsted-weight. The purse is shown in Bryspun kid-n-ewe (50% kid mohair, 50% wool; 120 yd [110 m]/50 g): #430, 3 skeins. Yarn was held double throughout.*

NEEDLES

Basic Everyday Purse: *Size 13 (9 mm), 24" (60 cm) circular needle and 2 double-pointed needles (dpn).* ***Basic Everyday Purse with flap:*** *Size 11 (8 mm), 24" (60 cm) circular needle.*

GAUGE

Unfelted Gauge

Basic Everyday Purse: *10 sts = 4"(10 cm) in Stockinette stitch (St st). Getting an exact gauge is not critical for this pattern.*
Purse with flap: *11 sts = 4" (10 cm) in Stockinette stitch (St st). Getting an exact gauge is not critical for this pattern.*

Felted Gauge

Basic Everyday Purse: *About 11½ sts and 20 rows = 4" (10 cm) in St st. Felted gauge will vary with the yarn used and the amount of felting.*
Purse with flap: *About 13 sts and 24 rows = 4" (10 cm). Felted gauge will vary with the yarn used and the amount of felting.*

NOTIONS

Basic Everyday Purse with flap: *Marker; tapestry needle; button; button loop.*

FELTING

Follow basic felting instructions on page 10 until bag is desired size.

Everyday Purse with Flap

This purse sports a fold-over flap. Fasten it with a fancy button or add a tassel for extra zip!

Body (see page 27 for materials)

With circular needle and a double strand of yarn, cast on 58 sts. Place marker and join, being careful not to twist sts. Work in rounds of St st (knit every rnd) for 40 rnds.

Dec rnd: K3, [k2tog, k5] 3 times, k2tog, k32—54 sts.

Next rnd: P25, k29.

Next rnd: Bind off 25 sts, knit to end of rnd.

Flap

(Worked back and forth in rows on 29 sts.)

Row 1: (WS) K2, purl to last 2 sts, k2.

Row 2: Knit.

Repeat Rows 1 and 2 six more times, then repeat Row 1 once more.

Dec row: (RS) K3 [k2tog, k5] 3 times, k2tog, k3—25sts.

Knit 2 rows of garter stitch. Bind off all sts, knitwise.

Strap

With dpn and a double strand of yarn, cast on 3 sts and work in I-cord (see Techniques, page 103) for about 66" (168 cm). Cut yarn and draw tail through sts. Pull together tightly and fasten off.

Finishing

Sew cast-on edge together to close the bottom of the bag. To attach the strap as shown, begin with the strap ends even with the bottom of the bag, pin strap to both side edges. Slip-stitch into place. Weave in loose ends on WS. After felting, sew button to the front of the purse. Make a button loop (see Closures, page 21) of elastic cord and sew it to the underside of the flap.

Pocket Purse

This purse has room for all your stuff and a pocket for things you need close at hand.

Body

With circular needle and a double strand of MC, cast on 70 sts. Place marker and join, being careful not to twist sts. Work in rounds of St st (knit every rnd) for 56 rnds.

Garter-Stitch Border

Rnd 1: Knit.

Rnd 2: Purl.

Repeat Rnds 1 and 2 three more times. Bind off all sts, knit-wise.

Pocket

With circular needle and a double strand of CC, cast on 27 sts. Work back and forth in rows.

Row 1: (WS) k2, purl to last 2 sts, k2.

Row 2: Knit.

Repeat Rows 1 and 2 for a total of 34 rows. Knit 6 rows for garter-stitch border. Bind off all stitches knitwise.

Straps (make 2)

With dpn and a double strand of CC, cast on 5 sts and work in I-cord (see Techniques, page 103) for 28" (71 cm). Cut yarn and draw tail through sts. Pull together tightly and fasten off. Make second strap the same.

Finishing

Sew cast-on edge together to close the bottom of the bag. Pin pocket to one side of tote, placing top of pocket about 3 to 3½" (7.5 to 9 cm) down from top of purse. Slip-stitch pocket in place on sides and bottom edge, leaving top open. Putting a piece of cardboard inside the purse while sewing will prevent stitches from catching the back of the bag.

Weave in loose ends on WS.

Straps may be stitched on before or after felting. Position the strap ends on each side of the bag above the pocket as shown. Sew buttons on each strap end after felting.

SIZE

Finished size in the yarn shown: 10" by 10½" (25.5 by 26.5 cm).

YARN

350 yards (320 meters) worsted-weight wool in main color (MC) and 175 yards (160 meters) of the same yarn in contrast color (CC). The purse is shown in Brown Sheep Nature Spun Worsted (245 yd [224 m]/100 gr): #N04 blue knight (color A), 2 skeins; and # N48 scarlet (color B), 1 skein. Yarn is used double throughout.

NEEDLES

Size 13 (9 mm), 24" (60 cm) circular and 2 double-pointed (dpn).

GAUGE

***Unfelted Gauge** 10 sts = 4" (10 cm) in Stockinette st (St st). Getting an exact gauge is not critical for this pattern.*
***Felted Gauge** About 13 sts and 22 rows = 4" (10 cm). Felted gauge will vary with the yarn used and the amount of felting.*

NOTIONS

Marker; tapestry needle; 4 buttons.

FELTING

Follow basic felting instructions on page 10 until bag is desired size.

Evening Bags with Pizzazz

Put some glamour into your felt! These bags are all made by combining a wool that felts easily with a nonfelting novelty yarn. The evening bag is both elegant and very quick to knit. Being small, it does not require a lot of yarn so it's great for trying out new combinations of novelty yarn and wool. See the sidebar, Playing with Novelty Yarns, for more details. The envelope clutch is perfect for a special evening out. Add a pretty gold or silver chain to use it as a shoulder purse.

Easy Evening Bag

Body

With circular needle, one strand of wool, and one strand of novelty yarn held together, cast on 44 sts. Place marker and join, being careful not to twist sts. Knit in rnds of St st (knit every rnd) for 25–30 rnds, or until you run out of novelty yarn.

PLAYING WITH NOVELTY YARNS

Many nonfelting novelty yarns can be held together with wool to create interesting colored and textured felted fabrics. The felted gauge will vary drastically from one combination to another (see page 9), and not every combination will result in a fabric that you like. Some yarns hold up better through the felting process than others. Felting a sample or small project is the only way to determine what works and what you like. A small purse is a good test project because the gauge is not critical and the amount of time and yarn used is small.

SIZE

The evening bag shown measures 7" by 6" (18 by 15 cm). Size will vary with yarn used and the amount of felting.

YARN

55 yards (50 meters) of novelty yarn and 75 yards (68.5 meters) of worsted-weight wool. Shown in Trendsetter Sorbet (80% viscose, 15% poly, 5% metal; 55 yd [50 m]/50 g): violets, 1 skein, and Brown Sheep Nature Spun worsted (245 yd [224 m]/100 g): #N01 pepper.

NEEDLES

Size 13 (9 mm), 16" (40 cm) circular needle.

NOTIONS

Marker; tapestry needle; about 40" (101.5 cm) or desired length of purchased cording or chain for strap.

GAUGE

***Unfelted Gauge** 10 sts = 4" (10 cm) in Stockinette st (St st). Getting an exact gauge is not critical for this pattern.*
***Felted Gauge** About 13 sts and 24 rows = 4" (10 cm). Gauge will vary with the yarn used and the amount of felting.*

FELTING

Follow basic felting instructions on page 10, until bag is desired size.

Garter-Stitch Border

Cut the novelty yarn and continue with a single strand of wool.
Rnd 1: Knit.
Rnd 2: Purl.
Repeat rnds 1 and 2 three more times. Bind off all sts, knitwise.

Finishing

Sew cast-on edge together for bottom seam. Weave in loose ends on WS.

Straps

Sew cording or chain to the inside of the bag after felting.

Envelope Clutch

Body

With circular needle, one strand of wool and one strand of novelty yarn held together, cast on 58 sts. Place marker and join, being careful not to twist sts. Knit in rounds of St st (knit every rnd) for 30 rnds. Drop novelty yarn, but do not cut. With wool only, k28, turn. Knit back across the same 28 sts, turn.

Bind off these 28 sts. Cut wool and fasten off.

Flap

(Worked back and forth in rows on 30 sts.)
With purl side facing, rejoin wool where the novelty yarn was left off.

Continue working with 1 strand of each yarn held together.
Row 1: K2, purl to last 2 sts, k2.
Row 2: Knit.
Repeat Rows 1 and 2 twelve more times, then repeat Row 1 once more. Cut novelty yarn. With wool only, knit 3 rows. Bind off all sts, knitwise. Cut yarn and fasten off.

Finishing

Choose either the knit or the purl side as the RS. Sew cast-on edge together to close the bottom of the bag. Weave in loose ends on the WS.

SIZE
Finished size in the yarn shown is about 8½" by 6" (21.5 by 15 cm).

YARN
100 yards (92 meters) of novelty yarn and 120 yards (110 meters) of worsted-weight wool. The turquoise bag is shown in Berroco Jewel FX (94% rayon, 6% metallic; 57 yd [52 m]/25 g): # 6910 alexandrites, 2 skeins; and Mannings Hawthorne Cottage English Leicester DK wool (100% wool; 189 yd [173 m]/3.5 oz): #325 teal, 1 skein. Red and black bag is shown in Trendsetter Dune (41% mohair, 30% acrylic, 12% viscose, 11% nylon, 6% metallic; 90 yd [82 m]/50 g): #84 fuchsia, 2 skeins; and Brown Sheep Nature Spun Worsted (245 yd [224 m]/100 g): # N01 pepper, 1 skein.

NEEDLES
Size 13 (9 mm), 16" (40 cm) circular.

NOTIONS
Marker; tapestry needle.

GAUGE
Unfelted Gauge *10 sts = 4" (10 cm) in Stockinette st (St st). Getting an exact gauge is not critical for this pattern.*
Felted Gauge *About 13 sts and 24 rows = 4" (10 cm). Gauge will vary with the yarn used and the amount of felting.*

FELTING
Follow basic felting instructions on page 10 until bag is desired size.

Totes with a Twist

Totes are the perfect answer for days when your necessities just won't fit into a purse. Make the totes in the yarns suggested or experiment with other weights or combinations of yarns.

"Fur" Trimmed Tote

You'll be the height of fashion toting this "fur" trimmed bag around town! The bag shown uses Fizz for its fur, but you can use any other extra-thick eyelash-type novelty yarn, or try a long-haired mohair instead. Mohair will give a slightly different, but still very furry look. If you are trying a new yarn combination, test it on a small gift bag before investing time and yarn in this larger tote.

Body

With a double strand of wool, cast on 60 sts. Place marker and join, being careful not to twist sts.

Knit in rnds of St st (knit every rnd) for 46 rnds. Cut 1 strand of wool and add 1 strand of novelty yarn to the remaining strand of wool. Continue with these 2 yarns held together.

SIZE

Finished size in the yarn shown 10½" by 12" (26.5 by 30.5 cm).

YARN

345 yards (315.5 meters) of heavy worsted-weight wool and 40 yards (36.5 meters) of an extra-thick eyelash-type yarn for tote and 60 yards (55 meters) of worsted-weight wool for strap. The tote shown was made in Naturally 10-ply Tussock Aran (85% wool, 15% polyester; 173 yd [158 m]/100 g): #164 charcoal tweed, 2 skeins; and SR Kertzer Fizz (100% polyester; 65 yd [59.5 m]/50 g): #10 black, 1 skein. The strap was made in Brown Sheep Nature Spun Worsted (245 yd [224 m]/100 g): #N01 pepper, 1 skein.

NEEDLES

Size 13 (9 mm), 24"(60 cm) circular and 2 double-pointed (dpn).

NOTIONS

Marker; tapestry needle.

GAUGE

Unfelted Gauge *10 sts and 14 rows = 4"(10 cm) in Stockinette st (St st).*
Felted Gauge *About 11½ sts and 20 rows = 4"(10 cm). Felted gauge will vary with the yarn used and the amount of felting.*

FELTING

Follow basic felting instructions on page 10 until bag is desired size.

Knit 1 rnd. Purl 12 rnds. Cut novelty yarn and continue with a single strand of wool.

Knit 2 rnds. Purl 1 rnd. Bind off all sts, knitwise.

Strap

With 2 strands of wool and dpn, cast on 3 sts and work in I-cord (see Techniques, page 103) for 72" (183 cm). Cut yarn and draw tail through sts. Pull together tightly and fasten off.

Finishing

Sew the cast-on edges together to close the bottom of the bag. Fold the strap in half. Pin the doubled strap ends to the inside of the bag at each side about 1½" (3.8 cm) down from the top. Check that the strap is not twisted, then slip-stitch the ends into place. Weave in loose ends on WS.

Tab-Top Tote

The flat bottom of this sturdy tote is reinforced with a second layer of felt. Make it in worsted-weight for a midsized bag, or choose bulky-weight yarn for a larger bag. This tote is great for carrying your current knitting project.

Bottom

With circular needle, loosely cast on 64 sts. Place marker and join, being careful not to twist sts.
Rnd 1: Purl.
Rnd 2: K1, *M1 (see Techniques, page 103), k1 and mark this st with a pin or split marker, M1, k28, M1, k1 and mark this st, M1,* k2; repeat from * to * once, end k1—72 sts.
Rnd 3: Purl.
Rnd 4: Knit to first marked st, M1, k1, M1, *knit to next marked st, M1, k1, M1; repeat from * 2 more times, knit to end of rnd—80 sts.
Repeat Rnds 3 and 4 until there are 104 sts. Purl 1 rnd.

SIZES
About 10" by 10½" (25.5 by 26.5 cm) in worsted-weight yarn; about 14½" by 12" (37 by 30.5 cm) in bulky-weight yarn.

YARN
350 yards (320 meters) of worsted-weight or 450 yards (411.5 meters) of bulky-weight. Always test your yarns to be sure that they felt to a nice fabric at the gauge given. The two totes shown are made in Baabajoes Woolpak 10-ply (worsted) (100% wool; 430 yd [393 m]/250 g): #HP-1 mountain, 1 skein; and Woolpak 14-ply (bulky) (100% wool; 310 yd [283.5 m]/250 g): #08 plum, 2 skeins.

NEEDLES
For worsted-weight: Size 10½ (6.5 mm), 24" (60 cm) circular and 2 double-pointed (dpn). For bulky-weight: Size 11 (8 mm), 24" (60 cm) circular and 2 double-pointed (dpn). For either yarn weight: a spare circular in size 9 (5.5 mm) or smaller.

NOTIONS
Markers: Split ring markers or coilless pins; stitch holders; tapestry needle.

GAUGE
Unfelted Gauge *Worsted-weight: 14 sts and 21 rows = 4" (10 cm) in Stockinette st (St st). Bulky-weight: 11 sts and 19 rows = 4" (10 cm) in Stockinette st (St st).*
Felted Gauge *Worsted-weight: About 20 sts and 29 rows = 4" (10 cm). Bulky-weight: About 15 sts and 26 rows = 4"(10 cm).*
Felted gauge will vary with the yarn used and the amount of felting.

FELTING
Follow basic felting instructions on page 10 until bag is desired size.

Body

Knit even in St st (knit every rnd) for 70 rnds. Adjust the number of rounds knitted to change the depth of the bag.

Tab Top (see Mid-row BO, Techniques, page 103)

Bind off 4 sts, knit 5 sts and place on holder, *bind off 8 sts, knit 5 sts and place on holder; repeat from * to last 4 sts, bind off 4 sts. Cut yarn and fasten off. Working on one set of 5 sts at a time, join yarn with WS facing. Knit 12 rows of garter stitch (knit every row) (6 ridges), ending with a RS row. Bind off all 5 sts. Cut yarn, leaving a tail long enough to sew tab down. Fold tab in half, WS together, and sew bound-off edge to inside of tote. Repeat for remaining tabs.

Second Bottom Piece

With circular needle, cast on 64 sts. Place marker and join, being careful not to twist sts. Work same as the first bottom until there are 104 sts. Purl 1 rnd. With spare smaller circular needle, pick up the top loops of the last purl round of the tote bottom. Place the second bottom piece on top of the tote bottom. Holding both needles in your left hand, and with the bottom of the bag facing, work a 3-needle bind off (see Techniques, page 103).

Strap

With dpn, cast on 3 sts and work in I-cord (see Techniques, page 103) for about 68" (173 cm). Cut yarn and draw tail through sts. Pull together tightly and fasten off.

Finishing

Working a flat seam (see Techniques, page 107), first sew the cast-on edges of the inner bottom piece together, then repeat for the second (outer) bottom. Using short and very loose stitches, tack the two bottoms together down the center. This will encourage them to felt together.

Weave in loose ends on WS. Thread strap through the tabs at the top of the tote, then sew the two strap ends together.

warm heads

Felted fabric lends itself perfectly to stylish hats. From classic-brimmed bowlers to jaunty berets, your head will always be toasty warm, even in the coldest weather. Felted knit hats have the added advantage of being both wind- and rain-resistant.

Brimmed Hats

Each of these hats is a classic. The first sports a narrow brim, the second has a shaped brim that gradually changes from less than 1" (2.5 cm) wide to 2¼" (5.5 cm wide. The I-cord hatband is an easy way to add a professional touch to either hat.

Narrow-Brim Style

Brim

With circular needle, cast on 110 sts. Place marker and join, being careful not to twist sts.
Rnd 1: Purl.
Rnd 2: Knit.
Knit 7 more rounds in St st (knit every rnd).

Shape Crown:
Rnd 1: *K2tog, k2tog, k1; repeat from *—66 sts.
Rnds 2 and 3: Knit.
Rnd 4: *K3, M1 (see Techniques, page 103); repeat from *—88 sts.
Knit 31 rounds even.

Shape Top:
(Change to dpn when necessary.)
Rnd 1: *K9, k2tog; repeat from *—80 sts.
Rnd 2 and all remaining even rnds: Knit.
Rnd 3: *K8, ssk; repeat from *—72 sts.
Rnd 5: *K7, k2tog; repeat from *—64 sts.
Rnd 7: *K6, ssk; repeat from *—56 sts.
Rnd 9: *K5, k2tog; repeat from *—48 sts.
Rnd 11: *K4, ssk; repeat from *—40 sts.
Rnd 13: *K3, k2tog; repeat from *—32 sts.
Rnd 15: *K2, ssk; repeat from *—24 sts.
Rnd 17: *K1, k2tog; repeat from *—16 sts.
Rnd 19: *Ssk; repeat from *—8 sts.
Cut yarn and draw tail through last 8 sts. Pull together tightly and fasten off.

Finishing

Weave in loose ends on WS.

SIZE
Average adult. The finished size is determined by felting time and blocking.

YARN
190 yards (174 meters) of a heavy worsted-weight yarn for hats, 15 yards (14 meters) each of a DK-weight alpaca or wool and a novelty yarn for hatband. Always test your yarns to be sure that they felt to a nice fabric at the gauge given. The narrow brimmed hat is shown in Brown Sheep Lamb's Pride Worsted (85% wool, 15% mohair; 190 yd [174 m]/4 oz): #M06 deep charcoal, 1 skein. The shaped brimmed hat is also shown in Lamb's Pride Worsted: #M29 jacks plum, 1 skein. Hatband shown on plum hat was knit in Blue Sky Alpaca (100% alpaca; 120 yd [110 m] 2 oz): #100 black, and Stacy Charles Ritratto (28% mohair, 53% rayon, 10% nylon, 9% poly; 198 yd [181 m] 50 g): #63 black/plum, 1 skein each.

NEEDLES
Size 10½ (6.5 mm), 24" (60 cm) circular and set of 4 double-pointed (dpn). Adjust needle size if necessary to obtain the correct gauge.

NOTIONS
Marker; tapestry needle.

GAUGE
Unfelted Gauge *14 sts and 18 rows = 4" (10 cm) in Stockinette stitch (St st).*
Felted Gauge *About 16½ sts and 30 rows = 4" (10 cm). Gauge will vary with the amount of felting.*

FELTING AND BLOCKING
Follow basic felting instructions on page 10 and block following the suggestions on pages 14 and 40. If you have made a hatband, felt it in a separate bag along with your hat. To block, first stretch the wet hat over your form, then stretch the band to fit over the hat. Leave both on the form until they are completely dry.

Shaped-Brim Style

Brim

With circular needle, cast on 110 sts. Place marker and join, being careful not to twist sts.
Rnd 1: Purl.
Rnd 2: Knit.

Shape Brim

Rnd 3: K22, M1 (see Techniques, page 103), *k11, M1; repeat to last 22 sts, k22—117 sts.
Rnd 4: Knit.
Work short rows (see Techniques, page 103) as follows:
Row 5: K75, wrap next st and turn (W&T).
Row 6: P33, W&T.
Row 7: K43, W&T.
Row 8: P53, W&T.
Row 9: K63, W&T.
Row 10: P73, W&T.
Row 11: K6, [k2tog, k8] 6 times, k2tog, k15, W&T.
Row 12: P86, W&T.
Row 13: Knit to marker at center back—110 sts remain.

FELTING AND BLOCKING HATS

Most hats have no special felting needs, other than the normal careful checking during the felting process. Blocking, however, plays an important role in the finishing of many styles.

To achieve a smooth crown on a brimmed hat, felt until it is slightly smaller than you desire, then stretch it over a hat form while wet. A bowl or ball, even a strong balloon, may be used in place of a hat form. Choose a form size that is just slightly larger than the intended wearer's head measurement, and be sure to leave the hat on the form until it is completely dry. If you need to wash your hat, repeat the blocking process.

Knit 2 complete rounds. Work the same as for Narrow-Brim Style, beginning with Shape Crown.

I-cord Band

With 2 dpn and 1 strand of DK weight alpaca or wool held with 1 strand of novelty yarn, cast on 3 sts. Work I-cord (see Techniques, page 103) for 30" (76 cm). Bind off and sew ends together to form a circle.

Felted Beret

This jaunty beret is perfect for when you're feeling stylish.

Band

Cut a length of elastic about 2" (5 cm) shorter than head measurement. Overlap ½" (1.3 cm) of the ends to make a circle and sew together securely. Set aside. With larger circular needle, loosely cast on 78 sts. Place marker and join, being careful not to twist sts.

Purl 6 rounds (rnds).

Using the spare smaller circular needle, pick up the lower loops of the cast-on edge—78 sts on spare needle. Fold the band in half, purl side out, with the spare needle behind the working needle.

Lay the loop of elastic between the needles. With larger circular needle, work 3-needle join (see Techniques, page 103), encasing the elastic in the band—78 sts.

Body

Inc Rnd: *K1, inc in each of next 2 sts; repeat from *—130 sts.
Knit 22 rnds even in St st (knit every rnd).

Shape Top:

(Change to dpn when necessary.)
Rnd 1 *K11, k2tog; repeat from *—120 sts.
Rnds 2–4: Knit.
Rnd 5: *K10, ssk; repeat from *—110 sts.
Rnds 6–8: Knit.
Rnd 9: *K9, k2tog; repeat from *—100 sts.
Rnds 10 and 11: Knit.
Rnd 12: *K8, ssk; repeat from *—90 sts.
Rnds 13 and 14: Knit.
Rnd 15: *K7, k2tog; repeat from *—80 sts.
Rnds 16 and 17: Knit.
Rnd 18: *K6, ssk; repeat from *—70 sts.
Rnds 19 and 20: Knit.

SIZE

Average adult. The finished size is determined by felting time. The band is sized with elastic encased in the felt.

YARN

200 yards (183 meters) of worsted-weight yarn. Always test your yarns to be sure that they felt to a nice fabric at the gauge given. The beret is shown in Green Mountain Spinnery Double Twist (100% wool; 250 yd [229 m]/4oz): #3 garnet, 1 skein; and Bryspun kid-n-ewe (50% kid mohair, 50% wool; 120 yd [110 m] 50 g): #340 teal, 2 skeins.

NEEDLES

Size 10 (6 mm), 24" (60 cm) circular and set of double-pointed (dpn); spare circular needle at least three sizes smaller than the working needle. Adjust needle sizes if necessary to obtain the correct gauge.

NOTIONS

¾ yd (.68 cm) of ¼-inch-wide (6 mm) elastic for band; marker.

GAUGE

Unfelted Gauge *15 sts and 20 rows = 4"(10 cm) in Stockinette stitch (St st).*
Felted Gauge *About 18½ sts and 32 rows = 4" (10 cm). Gauge will vary with the amount of felting.*

FELTING AND BLOCKING

Follow basic felting instructions on page 10. Berets do not require any special blocking unless you want a sharp crease in the top. In this case, stretch the top over an appropriate size plate. Otherwise, just smooth the fabric and lay on a towel to dry.

Rnd 21: *K5, k2tog; repeat from *—60 sts.
Rnds 22 and 23: Knit.
Rnd 24: *K4, ssk; repeat from *—50 sts.
Rnds 25 and 26: Knit.
Rnd 27: *K3, k2tog; repeat from *—40 sts.
Rnd 28: Knit.
Rnd 29: *K2, ssk; repeat from *—30 sts.
Rnd 30: Knit.
Rnd 31: *K1, k2tog; repeat from *—20 sts.
Rnd 32: Knit.
Rnd 33: *Ssk; repeat from *—10 sts.
Rnd 34: *K2tog; repeat from *—5 sts.

Finishing

Cut yarn and draw tail through last 5 sts. Pull together tightly and fasten off.

Weave in loose ends on WS.

Angora Baby Hat

This ultra-soft angora hat will keep your baby warm and toasty.

Band

With circular needle and beginning at rolled band, cast on 63 (70, 77) sts. Place marker and join, being careful not to twist sts.

Rnds 1–3: Knit in St st (knit every rnd).
Rnd 4: *K7, M1 (see Techniques, page 103); repeat from *—72 (80, 88) sts.
Rnds 5–7: Knit.
Rnd 8: *K4, M1; repeat from *—90 (100, 110) sts.
Rnds 9 –16: Knit.
Rnd 17: *K2tog, k2tog, k1, repeat from *—54 (60, 66) sts.

Note: The markers in the next round are for earflap placement. Disregard if you do not want earflaps.

Rnd 18: K6 (7, 7), mark last st worked with a pin or split marker, k12 (14, 16), mark last st worked, k19 (19, 21), mark last st worked, k12 (14, 16), mark last st worked, k5 (6, 6).
Rnd 19: Knit.
Rnd 20 (inc): *M1, k3; repeat from *—72 (80, 88) sts.

Body

Knit 20 (23, 26) rnds even.

Shape Top

(Change to dpn when necessary.)
Rnd 1: *K7 (8, 9), ssk; repeat from *—64 (72, 80) sts.
Rnd 2 and all remaining even numbered rnds: Knit.
Rnd 3: *K6 (7, 8), k2tog; repeat from *—56 (64, 72) sts.
Rnd 5: *K5 (6, 7), ssk; repeat from *—48 (56, 64) sts.
Rnd 7: *K4 (5, 6), k2tog; repeat from *—40 (48, 56) sts.
Rnd 9: *K3 (4, 5), ssk; repeat from *—32 (40, 48) sts.
Rnd 11: *K2 (3, 4), k2tog; repeat from *—24 (32, 40) sts.
Rnd 13: *K1 (2, 3), ssk; repeat from *—16 (24, 32) sts.
Rnd 15: *K0 (1, 2), k2tog; repeat from *—8 (16, 24) sts.
For sizes M and L only: *K(0, 1), ssk; repeat from *—(8, 16) sts.
For size L only: *K2tog; repeat from *—8 sts.

I-cord Top: (All sizes)

Row 1: [K2tog] 4 times, working all sts onto 1 dpn.
Row 2: Slide sts to the other end of the needle and taking yarn across the back, work k1, k2tog, k1—3 sts remain. Continue working I-cord (see Techniques, page 103) on these 3 sts until cord is 4" (10 cm) long, measuring from top of hat.
Next row: K1, k2tog.

SIZE

Small (medium, large); to fit about 3–6 (6–12, 12–24) months. Size is determined by the felting time and blocking. Hats will have a finished, blocked, crown diameter of about 15½ (17, 18½)" (39.5 [43, 47] cm).

YARN

135 (150, 170) yards (123.5 [137, 155.5] meters) of DK-weight angora/wool blend yarn. The angora hats are shown in Garnstudio Angora Tweed (70% merino, 30% angora; 158 yd [144.5 m]/50 g): #06 brown and #12 purple, 1 skein per hat.

NEEDLES

Size 8 (5 mm), 16" (40 cm) circular and set of 4 double-pointed (dpn). Adjust needle size if necessary to obtain the correct gauge.

NOTIONS

Markers; split ring markers or coilless pins; tapestry needle.

GAUGE

***Unfelted Gauge** 17 sts and 22 rows = 4" (10 cm) in Stockinette stitch (St st).*
***Felted Gauge** About 19 sts and 29 rows = 4" (10 cm). Gauge will vary with the amount of felting.*

FELTING AND BLOCKING

Follow basic felting instructions on page 10. If the final size needs to be a little larger, this hat may be blocked over a small bowl. If not, just smooth the fabric and set over a drinking glass so it will dry without creases. If desired, brush gently to fluff the angora after the hat is dry.

MY OWN CHAI

Last row: K2tog. Cut yarn and draw tail through last st. Pull together tightly and fasten off.

Earflaps

optional earflaps shown with short I-cord tassels
Work each earflap separately. Turn hat inside out and find the earflap markers on one side of the hat.

Use a dpn to pick up the top loop of the marked st and each st to the 2nd marked st—13 (15, 17) sts.

Join yarn and work back and forth in rows of garter st (knit every row) as follows:

Note: Slip all sts purlwise with yarn in front (wyif).

Row 1: (WS) K3, [inc in next st, k2 (3, 4)] twice, inc in next st, wyif, slip 3—16 (18, 20) sts.
Row 2: (RS) Knit to last 3 sts, wyif, slip 3.
Rows 3–11: Repeat row 2.
Row 12: K3, ssk, knit to last 5 sts, k2tog, wyif, slip 3—14 (16, 18) sts.
Rows 13, 14, and 15: Repeat row 2.
Repeat rows 12–15 until 8 sts remain.
Next row: (WS) K2, ssk, k1, wyif, slip 3, turn—7 sts.
Next row: K2, ssk, wyif, slip 3, turn—6 sts.
Next row: K1, k2tog, wyif, slip 3, turn—5 sts.
Last row: (RS) K1, k2tog, k2tog—3 sts. Do not turn.

Short I-cord Tassels

Slide sts to the other end of the needle.
Row 1: Knit 3. Slide sts to the other end of the dpn without turning. Repeat row 1 until I-cord measures 3" (7.5 cm) from the end of earflap. Cut yarn and draw tail through sts. Pull together tightly and fasten off.

To Finish Without Tassels

After last earflap row, cut yarn and draw through remaining 3 sts. Pull together tightly and fasten off. Make second earflap the same as the first.

Finishing

Weave in loose ends on WS. When felted and dry, tie a knot at the ends of the I-cord tassels and at the base of the top I-cord.

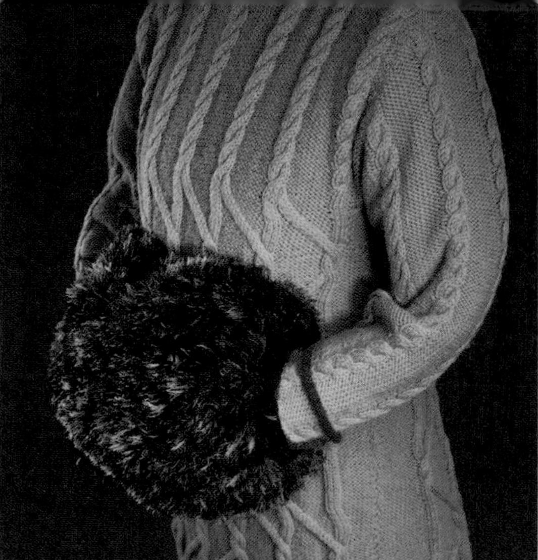

warm hands & heart

Felted mittens and vests are practical winter wear for everyone in the family, from toddlers to grandparents! To keep them from being too bulky, all the mittens but the toddler's are shaped to fit the curve of the hand. If you're using your mittens for outdoor work or for driving, consider sewing on suede palms. The suede adds extra grip and extends the life of the mittens. For warmth with an elegant flair, nothing beats a muff. Made in wool and novelty yarn, this muff is a modern twist on an old-fashioned classic. Once your hands are warm, you'll want a felted vest to keep the rest of you warm. This felted vest is worked seamlessly to the armholes and then divided for the back and the front. It features unisex sizing making it appropriate for both men and women.

mittens

PREPARING MITTENS FOR FELTING

It is sometimes hard to avoid a hole or two around the thumb gusset when you're working at a loose gauge on large needles. Be sure to darn the holes closed before felting, following the instructions on page 8. Always check your pattern for any special information, such as adding temporary cuffs.

FELTING AND BLOCKING MITTENS

Follow the basic felting instructions on page 10 for all the mitten patterns. Be sure to remove both mittens from the bag each time you do a progress check.

If you've made your mittens out of long-fiber yarns such as alpaca or mohair blends, pay careful attention to them during the early stages of the felting process. As the long fibers felt, the insides of the mittens may begin to stick together. This is much easier to avoid than to fix after the fact. Within 10 minutes or less of starting the felting process, take the mittens out of the washer and slip your hands inside both of them, paying special attention to the thumbs. If you notice fibers beginning to stick together, check the mittens more frequently. For toddler's and children's mittens, use a wooden spoon handle to be sure the thumb stays open. (See page 16 for more information on what to do if your item isn't felting as expected.)

For final shaping and to customize the fit, use your hands or the intended wearer's hands to help mold the wet felt. Mittens dry faster on a mitten drying rack. If you don't have one, you can make a temporary rack out of long-handled spoons in a heavy vase.

ADDING CUFFS AFTER FELTING

Both the toddler's and children's mitten patterns have cuffs that are knitted on after felting. Waiting until after felting to add the cuffs allows for a snug fit to help hold mittens on little hands. See the sidebar on combining felted and unfelted knitting on page 50.

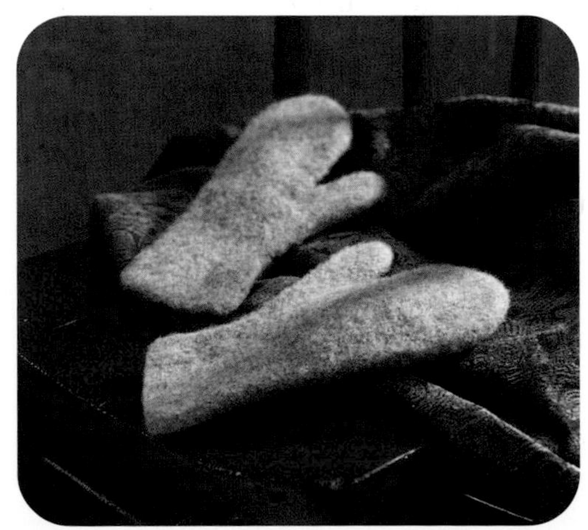

Toddler's Mittens

Made in an angora blend, these mittens add a soft touch of luxury to any little one's winter wardrobe.

Note: Right and left mittens are the same.

With larger dpn, cast on 26 (28) sts. Arrange sts evenly on 3 dpn, place marker and join, being careful not to twist sts. Knit 2 (3) rnds in St st (knit every rnd).

Thumb Gusset

Rnd 1: M1 (see Techniques, page 103), k2, M1, knit to end of rnd—28 (30) sts.
Rnds 2 and 3: Knit.
Rnd 4: M1, k4, M1, knit to end of rnd—30 (32) sts.
Rnds 5 and 6: Knit.
Rnd 7: M1, k6, M1, knit to end of rnd—32 (34) sts.
Rnds 8 and 9: Knit.
Rnd 10: M1, k8, M1, knit to end of rnd—34 (36) sts.
Knit 1 (2) rnds even.

Divide for Thumb Opening

Next rnd: M1, slip next 10 sts to a holder for thumb, M1, knit to end of rnd—26 (28) sts. Knit 10 (13) rnds even in St st.

Shape Top

Rnd 1: *Ssk, k11 (5); repeat from *—24 sts.
Rnd 2: Knit.
Rnd 3: *K2, k2tog; repeat from *—18 sts.
Rnds 4 and 5: Knit.
Rnd 6: *K1, ssk; repeat from *—12 sts.
Rnd 7: Knit.
Rnd 8: *K2tog; repeat from *—6 sts. Cut yarn and draw tail through remaining sts. Pull together tightly and fasten off.

Thumb

Slip the 10 sts from the holder onto 1 dpn. With 2nd dpn, pick up 2 sts from body of mitten—12 sts. Arrange sts evenly on 3 dpn, place marker before first

SIZES

Medium (large); to fit about 12 (24) months when felted to a finished length of about 3¾" (4¼") (9.5 [11] cm), excluding ribbing. Size can be adjusted up or down by the amount of felting.

CAUTION

These mittens are not recommended for small infants. All natural fibers, and angora in particular, will shed even when felted.

YARN

60 (75) yards (55 [68.5] meters) of DK-weight yarn that will felt to the gauge given plus 25 yd of the same, or a similar, weight yarn for cuffs. Always test your yarns to be sure that they felt to a nice fabric at the gauge given. Toddler's mittens are shown in Garnstudio, Angora Tweed, (70% merino, 30% angora; 158 yd [144.5 m]/50 g): #06 brown, 1 skein. Cuffs, applied after felting, are Blue Sky Alpaca, (100% alpaca; 120 yd [110 m]/50 g): #05 taupe, 1 skein.

NEEDLES

Size 8 (5 mm) and size 3 (3.25 mm) set of 4 double-pointed (dpn). Adjust needle size if necessary to obtain the correct gauge.

NOTIONS

Marker; stitch holder; tapestry needle; about 10 yd (9 m) of sport-weight, waste cotton.

GAUGE

***Unfelted** 17 sts and 23 rows = 4" (10 cm) in Stockinette st (St st) on larger needles.*
***Felted** About 19 sts and 29 rows = 4" (10 cm). Gauge will vary with the amount of felting.*

FELTING AND FINISHING

Follow basic felting instructions on page 10 and notes on mitten felting at the beginning of this section. Tiny mittens may take longer to felt than larger sizes. It is helpful to turn them inside out every other time you do a progress check, and it is especially important to add a heavy item to the wash to increase agitation.

picked up stitch and join yarn at this point.
Knit 8 (9) rnds.
1st Dec rnd: *K1, k2tog; repeat from *—8 sts.
Knit 1 rnd even.
2nd Dec rnd: *Ssk; repeat from *—4 sts. Cut yarn and draw tail through remaining sts. Pull together tightly and fasten off.

Finishing

Weave in loose ends on WS. Check for holes and mend if necessary. With smaller dpn and waste cotton, pick up and knit 26 (28 sts) from cast on edge. (See sidebar at right.) Knit 2 rnds then bind off. Tie both ends of waste yarn together and trim excess.

Cuff

Worked after mittens are felted and dry.
With smaller dpn and cuff yarn, pick up and knit 1 st in the base of each cotton st—26 (28) sts. Cut and remove waste cotton. Work in k1, p1 ribbing for 2" (5 cm), or desired length. Bind off very loosely knitwise. (Use a larger needle for binding off if necessary to keep the sts loose.) Cut yarn, fasten off, and weave in all loose ends on WS, noting that if cuff is to be turned back, the inside is the exposed side.

Combining Felted and Unfelted Knitting

Adding an unfelted ribbing, cuff, or trim to a felted item is easy to do, and it only requires a little preparation ahead of time. (This technique is used to add the contrasting bands to the vest on page 62 and you can use it to add knit bands or trim to any of your felt projects.) First, stabilize the edge of your item with a nonfelting yarn so it won't flare during the felting process. To do this knit a temporary edging using a waste cotton yarn that is about the same weight as the yarn you intend to use for the knitted band. This will also mark the placement of stitches to pick up later. Be sure the cotton you choose is colorfast (white or cream is best). Using the same size needle you intend to use for the trim, with the waste cotton, pick up and knit the exact number of stitches you will need and knit at least two rows. Bind off.

Felt your item and allow it to dry completely. Do not remove the cotton just yet, because the holes will quickly disappear. Using your edging yarn, pick up one stitch at the base of each cotton stitch, then cut and remove the cotton and continue knitting until your edging is the length you desire.

Child's Mittens

Wool is warm even when wet, so felted mittens mean warm hands no matter how many snowmen you build!

Right Mitten

With larger dpn, cast on 30 (32, 34) sts very loosely.
Arrange sts evenly onto 3 dpn, place marker and join being careful not to twist sts.
Knit 1 (2, 2) rnds in St st (knit every rnd).

Thumb Gusset

Rnd 1: M1 (see Techniques, page 103), k3, M1, knit to end of rnd—32 (34, 36) sts.
Rnds 2 and 3: Knit.
Rnd 4: M1, k5, M1, knit to end of rnd—34 (36, 38) sts.
Rnds 5 and 6: Knit.
Rnd 7: M1, k7, M1, knit to end of rnd—36 (38, 40) sts.
Rnds 8 and 9: Knit.
Rnd 10: M1, k9, M1, knit to end of rnd—38 (40, 42) sts.
Rnds 11 and 12: Knit.
Rnd 13: M1, k11, M1, knit to end of rnd—40 (42, 44) sts.
Knit 1 (2, 3) rnds even.

Divide for Thumb Opening

Next rnd: K1, place the next 11 sts on a holder, cast on 3 sts, knit to end of rnd—32 (34, 36) sts.

Body

Knit 2 (3, 4) rnds even.
Work short rows (see Techniques, page 103) as follows:
1st Short-row: K3, wrap next st and turn (W&T), p22 (23, 24), W&T, k19 (20, 21), ending at marker.
Knit 3 (4, 5) rnds even, knitting the wraps with the st they wrap on the first rnd.
2nd Short-row: K2, W&T, p20 (21, 22), W&T, k18 (19, 20), ending at marker.
Knit 3 (4, 5) rnds even.
3rd Short-row: K1, W&T, p18 (19, 20), W&T, k17 (18, 19) ending at marker.
Knit 2 (3, 4) rnds even.

SIZES

Small (medium, large). Designed to be felted to a finished length of about 5" (5¾", 6½") (12.5 [14.5, 16.5] cm) excluding ribbing. Size can be adjusted up or down by the amount of felting

YARN

95 (105, 125) yards (87 [96, 114] meters) of DK-weight wool that will felt to the gauge given. Cuffs require about 30 (35, 40) yards (27.5 [32, 36.5] meters) of matching or contrasting yarn of a similar weight. Always test your yarns to be sure that they felt to a nice fabric at the gauge given. Mittens are shown in Dale of Norway's Heilo (100% wool; 109 yd [100 m]/50 g): #5264 purple and #4137 red, 1 (1, 2) balls. Cuffs are knit in Bryspun kid-n-ewe (50% kid mohair, 50% wool; 120 yd [110 m] 50 g): #480 purple, 1 ball.

NEEDLES

Size 9 (5.5 mm) and size 3 (3.25 mm) set of 4 double-pointed (dpn). Adjust needle size if necessary to obtain the correct gauge.

NOTIONS

Marker; stitch holder; tapestry needle; about 15 yd (14 m) of sport-weight, waste cotton.

GAUGE

***Unfelted** 17 sts and 22 rows = 4" (10 cm) in Stockinette st (St st) on larger needle.*
***Felted** About 21 sts and 32 rows = 4" (10 cm). Gauge will vary with the amount of felting.*

FELTING AND FINISHING

Follow basic felting instructions on page 10 and notes on mitten felting at the beginning of this section. Small mittens may take longer to felt than larger sizes. It is helpful to turn them inside out every other time you do a progress check, and it is especially important to add a heavy item to the wash to increase agitation.

Shape Top

Rnd 1: *Ssk, k6 (15, 7); repeat from *—28 (32, 32) sts.
Rnds 2 and 3: Knit.
Rnd 4: *K2, k2tog; repeat from—21 (24, 24) sts.
Rnds 5 and 6: Knit.
Rnd 7: *K1, ssk; repeat from *—14 (16, 16) sts.
Rnd 8: Knit.
Rnd 9: *K2tog; repeat from *—7 (8, 8) sts. Cut yarn and draw tail through remaining sts. Pull together tightly and fasten off.

Thumb

Slip the 11 sts from holder onto dpn. With second dpn, pick up 5 sts around thumbhole—16 sts. Arrange sts evenly on 3 dpn, place marker before first picked up stitch and join yarn at this point.
Knit 2 (3, 4) rnds even.
1st Dec rnd: Ssk, k1, k2tog, knit to end of rnd—14 sts.
Knit 6 (7, 7) rnds even.
2nd Dec rnd: [K1, k2tog, k2, k2tog] 2 times—10 sts.
Knit 1 rnd even.
3rd Dec rnd: *K2tog; repeat from *—5 sts. Cut yarn and draw tail through remaining sts. Pull together tightly and fasten off.

Left Mitten

Work the same as for right mitten to beginning of thumb gusset.

Thumb Gusset

Rnd 1: K27 (29, 31), M1, k3, M1—32 (34, 36) sts.
Rnds 2 and 3: Knit.
Rnd 4: K27 (29, 31), M1, k5, M1—34 (36, 38) sts.
Rnds 5 and 6: Knit.
Rnd 7: K27 (29, 31), M1, k7, M1—36 (38, 40) sts.
Rnds 8 and 9: Knit.
Rnd 10: K27 (29, 31), M1, k9, M1—38 (40, 42) sts.
Rnds 11 and 12: Knit.
Rnd 13: K27 (29, 31), M1, k11, M1—40 (42, 44) sts.
Knit 1 (2, 3) rnds even.

Divide for Thumb Opening

Next rnd: K28 (30, 32), place the next 11 sts on a holder, cast on 3 sts, k1—32 (34, 36) sts.

Body

Knit 2 (3, 4) rnds even. Work short rows as follows:
1st Short-row: K19 (20, 21), W&T, p22 (23, 24), W&T, k3, ending at marker.
Knit 3 (4, 5) rnds even, knitting the wraps with the st they wrap on the first rnd.
2nd Short-row: K18 (19, 20), W&T, p20 (21, 22), W&T, k2, ending at marker.
Knit 3 (4, 5) rnds even.
3rd Short-row: K17 (18, 19), W&T, p18 (19, 20), W&T, k1, ending at marker.
Knit 2 (3, 4) rnds even. Shape top and knit thumb the same as for right mitten.

Finishing

Weave in loose ends on WS. Check for holes and mend if necessary. Using smaller dpn and waste cotton, pick up and knit 30 (32, 34) sts from cast on edge. Knit 2 rnds then bind off. Tie both ends of waste yarn together and trim excess.

Rib Cuff

(Worked after mittens are felted and dry.)
With smaller dpn and cuff yarn, pick up and knit 1 st in the base of each cotton st—30 (32, 34) sts. Cut and remove waste cotton. Work in k1, p1 ribbing for 3" (7.5 cm), or desired length. Bind off very loosely knitwise. (Use a larger needle for binding off if necessary to keep the sts loose.) Cut yarn, fasten off, and weave in loose ends on WS, noting that if cuff is to be turned back, the inside is the exposed side.

Cuff Variation

Work the same as for ribbed cuff, 10 rounds. Change to main color, purl 1 round then knit 6 rounds. Change back to contrasting color, purl 1 round then work in ribbing for 10 rounds. Follow Rib Cuff instructions above for bind off and finishing.

Adult's Mittens

Felted mittens have been known to encourage even the most grown-up adult to play in the snow!

Right Mitten

With dpn, loosely cast on (32, 36, 36)[40, 44] sts. Arrange sts evenly onto 3 dpn, place marker and join being careful not to twist sts. Work in k2, p2, ribbing for (16, 17, 18)[20] rnds.

For Women's size M and Men's size XL only: *Next rnd :* *K(16)[20], k2tog; repeat from *—(34)[42] sts.

All sizes: Knit (1, 1, 3)[2] rnds even in St st (knit every rnd).

Thumb Gusset

Rnd 1: K1, M1 (see Techniques, page 103), k3, M1, knit to end of rnd—(34, 36, 38)[42, 44] sts.

Rnds 2 and 3: Knit.

Rnd 4: K1, M1, k5, M1, knit to end of rnd—(36, 38, 40)[44, 46] sts.

Rnds 5 and 6: Knit.

Rnd 7: K1, M1, k7, M1, knit to end of rnd—(38, 40, 42)[46, 48] sts.

Rnds 8 and 9: Knit.

Rnd 10: K1, M1, k9, M1, knit to end of rnd—(40, 42, 44)[48, 50] sts.

Rnds 11 and 12: Knit.

Rnd 13: K1, M1, k11, M1, knit to end of rnd—(42, 44, 46)[50, 52] sts.

Rnds 14 and 15: Knit.

Rnd 16: K1, M1, k13, M1, knit to end of rnd—(44, 46, 48)[52, 54] sts.

Knit (1, 2, 3)[2] rnds even.

For Men's sizes only: *Next rnd:* K1, M1, k15, M1, knit to end of rnd—[54, 56] sts.

Knit 2 rnds even.

SIZES

Women's sizes are given first; men's sizes follow in [ ]. If there is only one figure or set of instructions, it applies to all sizes. ***Women's*** *(small, medium, large). These mittens are designed to be felted to a finished length of about 7" (7¾", 8½") (18 [19.5, 21.5] cm) excluding ribbing. Size can be adjusted up or down by the amount of felting.* ***Men's*** *[average, extra large]. The average size can be felted to fit most men's hands. These mittens measure 9" (23 cm) excluding ribbing, but they could be felted more or less, as needed, to fit. The extra large size is designed to be slightly longer and has a wider thumb and body. For a men's size small, use the instructions for women's size large.*

YARN

(160, 180, 210)[240, 275] yards (146.5, 164.5, 192)[219.5, 251.5] meters) of worsted-weight yarn that will felt to the gauge given. Always test your yarns to be sure that they felt to a nice fabric at the gauge given. Women's mittens are shown in Baabajoes 10-ply Woolpak (100% wool; 430 yd [394 m]/250 g): #33 bluebell and #31 softsun, 1 skein per pair. Men's mittens are shown in Green Mountain Spinnery 2 ply (100% wool; 250 yd [229 m]/100 g): chestnut, 1 skein.

NEEDLES

Size 10 (6 mm) set of 4 double-pointed (dpn). Adjust needle size if necessary to obtain the correct gauge. A size 10 (6mm) 16" (40 cm) circular needle may be used for the body of these mittens.

NOTIONS

Marker; stitch holder; tapestry needle; optional: suede palms.

GAUGE

Unfelted *14 sts and 21 rows = 4" (10 cm) in Stockinette st (St st).*
Felted *About 19 sts and 28 rows = 4" (10 cm). Gauge will vary with the amount of felting.*

FELTING

Follow basic felting instructions on page 10 and notes on mitten felting at the beginning of this section. Due to their long narrow shape, larger mittens may tend to stretch lengthwise, especially during the first stages of felting. To counteract this stretching, pull widthwise each time you do a progress check.

For Men's size XL only: *Next rnd:* K1, M1, k17, M1, knit to end of rnd—[58] sts. Knit 1 rnd even.

Divide for Thumb Opening

All sizes: *Next rnd:* K2, place the next (13)[15, 17] sts on a holder, cast on 3 sts, knit to end of rnd—(34, 36, 38)[42, 44] sts.

Body

Knit (2, 2, 3)[3, 4] rnds even. Work short rows (see Techniques, page 103) as follows:
1st Short-row: K4, wrap next st and turn (W&T), p(25, 26, 27)[29, 30], W&T, k(21, 22, 23)[25, 26], ending at marker.
Knit (3, 4, 5)[5] rnds even, knitting the wraps with the st they wrap on the first rnd.
2nd Short-row: K3, W&T, p(23, 24, 25)[27, 28], W&T, k(20, 21, 22)[24, 25], ending at marker.
Knit (3, 4, 4)[5] rnds even.
3rd Short-row: K2, W&T, p(21, 22, 23)[25, 26], W&T, k(19, 20, 21)[23, 24] ending at marker.
Knit (3, 4, 4)[5] rnds even.
4th Short-row: K1, W&T, p(19, 20, 21)[23, 24], W&T, k(18, 19, 20)[22, 23], ending at marker.
Knit (1, 2, 3)[2, 3] rnds even.

Shape Top

For Men's sizes only: *1st Dec rnd:* *Ssk, k[17, 18], k2tog; repeat from * once more—[38, 40] sts.
For Men's sizes only: Knit 1 rnd even.
For Men's sizes only: *2nd Dec rnd:* *Ssk, k[15, 16], k2tog; repeat from * once more —[34, 36] sts.
For Men's sizes only: Knit 1 rnd even.
All sizes: *1st [3rd]Dec rnd:* *Ssk, k(13, 14, 15)[13, 14], k2tog; repeat from * once more —(30, 32, 34)[30, 32] sts. Knit (2)[1] rnds even.
2nd [4th] Dec rnd: *Ssk, k(11, 12, 13)[11, 12], k2tog; repeat from * once more—(26, 28, 30)[26, 28] sts.
Knit 1 rnd even.
3rd [5th] Dec rnd: *Ssk, k(9, 10, 11)[9, 10], k2tog; repeat from * once more—(22, 24, 26)[22, 24] sts.
Knit 1 rnd even.

4th [6th] Dec rnd: *Ssk, k1, ssk, k(1, 2, 3)[1, 2], k2tog, k1, k2tog; repeat from * once more—(14, 16, 18)[14, 16] sts.
5th [7th] Dec rnd: *K2tog; repeat from *—(7, 8, 9)[7, 8] sts. Cut yarn and draw tail through remaining sts. Pull together tightly and fasten off.

Thumb

Slip the (13)[15, 17] sts from holder onto dpn. With second dpn, pick up 5 sts around thumbhole—(18)[20, 22] sts. Arrange sts evenly on 3 dpn. Place marker before first picked up stitch and join yarn at this point.
Knit (3, 4, 5)[6, 7] rnds even.
1st Dec rnd: Ssk, k1, k2tog, knit to end of rnd—(16)[18, 20] sts.
Knit 8 rnds even.
2nd Dec rnd: *K(2)[1], k2tog; repeat from * ending men's XL with k2—(12)[12, 14] sts.
Knit 1 rnd even.
3rd Dec rnd: *K2tog; repeat from *—(6)[6, 7] sts. Cut yarn and draw tail through remaining sts. Pull together tightly and fasten off.

Left Mitten

Work the same as for right mitten to beginning of thumb gusset.

Thumb Gusset

Rnd 1: K(28, 30, 32)[36, 38], M1, k3, M1, k1—(34, 36, 38)[42, 44] sts.
Rnds 2 and 3: Knit.
Rnd 4: K(28, 30, 32)[36, 38], M1, k5, M1, k1—(36, 38, 40)[44, 46] sts.
Rnds 5 and 6: Knit.
Rnd 7: K(28, 30, 32)[36, 38], M1, k7, M1, k1—(38, 40, 42)[46, 48] sts.
Rnds 8 and 9: Knit.
Rnd 10: K(28, 30, 32)[36, 38], M1, k9, M1, k1—(40, 42, 44)[48, 50] sts.
Rnds 11 and 12: Knit.
Rnd 13: K(28, 30, 32)[36, 38], M1, k11, M1, k1—(42, 44, 46)[50, 52] sts.
Rnds 14 and 15: Knit.
Rnd 16: K(28, 30, 32)[36, 38], M1, k13, M1, k1—(44, 46, 48)[52, 54] sts.
Knit (1, 2, 3)[2] rnds even.
For Men's sizes only: *Next rnd*: K[36, 38], M1, k15, M1, k1—[54, 56] sts.
Knit 2 rnds even.
For Men's size XL only: *Next rnd:* K[38], M1, k17, M1, k1—58 sts.
Knit 1 rnd even.

Divide for Thumb Opening

All sizes: Next rnd: K(29, 31, 33)[37, 39], place the next (13) [15, 17] sts on a holder, cast on 3 sts, k2—(34, 36, 38)[42, 44] sts.

Body

Knit (2, 2, 3)[3, 4] rnds even. Work short rows as follows:
1st Short row: K(21, 22, 23)[25, 26], W&T, p(25, 26, 27)[29, 30], W&T, k4, ending at marker.
Knit (3, 4, 5)[5] rnds even, knitting the wraps with the st they wrap on the first rnd.
2nd Short-row: K(20, 21, 22)[24, 25], W&T, p(23, 24, 25)[27, 28], W&T, k3, ending at marker.
Knit (3, 4, 4)[5] rnds even.
3rd Short-row: K(19, 20, 21)[23, 24], W&T, p(21, 22, 23)[25, 26], W&T, k2, ending at marker.
Knit (3, 4, 4)[5] rnds even.
4th Short-row: K(18, 19, 20)[22, 23], W&T, p(19, 20, 21)[23, 24], W&T, k1, ending at marker.
Knit (1, 2, 3)[2, 3] rnds even. Shape top and knit thumb the same as for right mitten.

Finishing

Weave in loose ends on WS. Check for holes and mend if necessary.

Fur-Cuffed Mittens

Dress up your mittens with a "fur" cuff by adding a thick eyelash-type novelty yarn before felting. Make these mittens along with the matching tote on page 33.

Note: Cuffs are the same for both right and left mitten.

Cuffs

With larger circular needle and a double strand of worsted-weight yarn, cast on 30 (30, 32) sts. Place marker and join being careful not to twist sts. Cut 1 strand of wool and add 1 strand of novelty yarn. Cuff is worked with these 2 yarns held together.

Rnds 1–4: Knit in rnds of St st (knit every rnd).
Rnd 5: [K13 (13, 14), k2tog] twice—28 (28, 30) sts. *Rnds 6–9:* Knit.
Rnd 10: [K12 (12, 13), k2tog] twice—26 (26, 28) sts. *Rnds 11–14:* Knit.
Rnd 15: [K11 (11, 12), k2tog] twice—24 (24, 26) sts.
Rnds 16–19: Knit. Cut novelty yarn and continue with 1 strand of worsted-weight yarn. Change to the smaller needles (circular or double-pointed).
Rnd 20: Knit.
Rnd 21: Size S only: *K3, M1 [see Techniques, page 103); repeat from *—32 sts.
Size M only: K2, M1, *k2, M1, k3, M1; repeat from * to last 2 sts, k2, M1—34 sts.
Size L only: K3, M1, *k3, M1, k2, M1; repeat from * to last 3 sts, k3, M1—36 sts.
All sizes: Knit 1 (2, 3) rnds even.

Follow women's mitten pattern on page 53 from the beginning of the thumb gusset, making a right and left mitten.

SIZES

Small (medium, large). Designed to be felted to a finished length of about 7" (7¾", 8½") (18 [19.5, 21.5] cm) excluding cuff. Size can be adjusted up or down by the amount of felting. Cuff measures about 3¾" (9.5 cm) long.

YARN

190 (210, 235) yards (174 [192, 215] meters) of worsted-weight yarn that will felt to the gauge given and 45 (45, 50) yards (41 [41, 46] meters) of an extra-thick, eyelash-type, novelty yarn.
Always test your yarns to be sure that they felt to a nice fabric at the gauge given. It is also very important to test felt a sample of wool with your novelty yarn to be sure it creates the look you want.
Mittens are shown in Naturally Tussock Aran 10 ply (85% wool, 15% polyester; 173 yd [158 m]/100 g): #164 charcoal tweed, 1 skein; and SR Kertzer Fizz (100% polyester; 65 yd [59.5 m]/50 g): #10 black.

NEEDLES

Size 11 (8 mm), 16" (40 cm) circular needle and size 10 (6 mm) set of double-pointed (dpn). A size 10 (6mm), 16" (40 cm) circular needle may be used for the body of these mittens.

NOTIONS

Markers; tapestry needle.

GAUGE

***Unfelted** 14 sts and 21 rows = 4" (10 cm) in Stockinette st (St st) on smaller needle with single strand of wool.*
***Felted** About 19 sts and 28 rows = 4" (10 cm). Gauge will vary with the amount of felting.*

FELTING

Follow basic felting instructions on page 10 and notes on mitten felting at the beginning of this section. The weight of the novelty yarn cuffs may cause your mittens to stretch lengthwise during the first stages of felting. This stretching is easy to counteract by slipping your hand inside each mitten and pulling it out widthwise every time you do a progress check. Since the novelty yarn will slow the felting process, the cuffs will not felt as firmly as the mittens. Don't be alarmed by the matted look of the Fizz when it is wet; it will fluff with just a good shake once it is dry.

Muff

This elegant alternative to mittens or gloves is reminiscent of days gone by.

First Cuff

With a single strand of wool and smaller circular needle, cast on 44 sts. Place marker and join, being careful not to twist sts.
Rnd 1: Purl
Rnd 2: Knit. Repeat rnds 1– 2 five more times—6 garter st ridges.

Body

Join 1 strand of novelty yarn and hold along with the strand of wool. Change to larger circular needle.
Inc rnd: *K4, M1 (see Techniques, page 103); repeat from *—55 sts. Work even in St st (knit every rnd) until muff measures 19" (48.5 cm) from cast on edge. Cut novelty yarn and continue with a single strand of wool.

Second Cuff

Rnd 1: With smaller circular needle, knit.
Rnd 2: *K3, k2tog; repeat from *—44 sts.
Rnd 3: Purl.
Rnd 4: Knit. Repeat rnds 3–4 four more times, then repeat rnd 3 once more—6 garter st ridges. Bind off loosely knitwise.

Wrist Cord

(optional)
With a single strand of wool and 2 dpn, cast on 3 sts. Work in I-cord (see Techniques, page 103) for 17" (43 cm).
Cut yarn and draw tail through 3 sts. Pull together tightly and fasten off. Thread one end of the I-cord between 2 sts at the top of the cuff (where novelty yarn begins). Sew the 2 ends of the I-cord together to form a loop.

Finishing

Weave in loose ends on WS.

FINISHED MEASUREMENTS
Designed to be felted to a finished length of about 13" (33 cm) excluding wrist cord and 21" (53.5 cm) circumference. Size will vary with the amount of felting.

YARN
210 yards (192 meters) worsted-weight wool and 150 yards (137 meters) of extra-thick eyelash-type novely yarn.
The muff is shown in Brown Sheep Nature Spun (100% wool; 245 yd [224 m] 100 g): #601 pepper and Berroco Zap (100% polyester; 50 yd [46 m]/50 g): #3440, 3 skeins.

NEEDLES
Size 10 (6 mm), 16" (40 cm) circular and 2 double-pointed (dpn); and size 11 (8 mm) 24" (60 cm) circular.

NOTIONS
Markers; tapestry needle.

GAUGE
Unfelted *10 sts and 15 rows = 4" (10 cm) with 1 strand of wool and 1 strand of novelty yarn on larger needles in Stockinette st (St st).*
Felted *About 12½ sts and 20 rows = 4" (10 cm).*

FELTING
Follow basic felting instructions on page 10, felting until desired size.

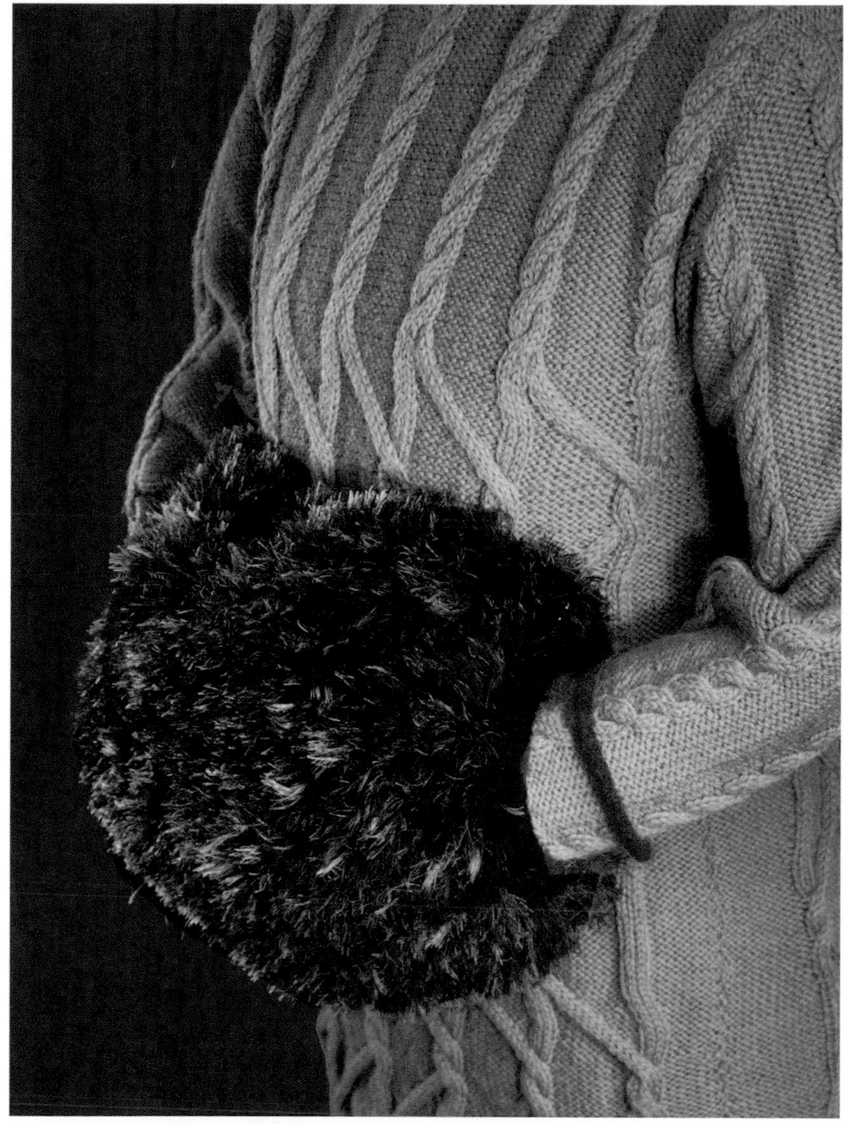

Felted Vest

Warm heads, warm hands, and now a warm heart! This felted vest is worked seamlessly to the armholes and then divided for the back and the front.

Back and Front

With larger needle, loosely cast on 146 (168, 190) sts. *Do not join.* Work back and forth in rows. Work 8 rows in garter st (knit every row). Purl 1 row.

Next row: (RS) K3 (2, 1), M1 (see Techniques, page 103), *k4, M1; repeat from * to last 3 (2, 1) sts, k3 (2, 1)—182 (210, 238) sts. Beginning with a purl row, work 96 (106, 110) rows in St st (knit on RS, purl on WS).

Divide for Armholes

(see Mid-row BO, Techniques, page 103)

Next Row: (WS) P37 (43, 49) for left front and place

SIZES

Finished chest measurement of about 38" (44", 50") (96.5 [112, 127] cm) and length of 24" (26", 27") (61 [66, 68.5] cm). Measurements are for worsted-weight yarn that is felted to the gauge specified in these instructions. Finished measurements will vary with the amount of felting. Since you are in control of the shrinkage, it is easy to stop the process when the vest is an inch or two larger than these measurements, or to felt it down slightly smaller.

YARN

Vest: *875 (1,050, 1,200) yards (800 [960, 1,097] meters) of worsted-weight wool.* ***Borders and collar:*** *About 200 (240, 260) yards (183 [219.5, 238] meters) of the same weight yarn in a contrasting or matching color. (This yarn need not be feltable wool as the borders are knit on after the vest is felted.) Vests shown are made with Baabajoes 10-ply Woolpak (100% wool; 430 yd [393 m]/250 g). The first vest is shown in #HP-1 mountain, with #06, plum, trim, the second vest is shown in #12 forest, with #10 black, trim; each using 3 skeins of main yarn and 1 skein for trim.*

NEEDLES

Size 10 (6 mm), 32" (80 cm) circular for body and size 7 (4.5 mm), 24" (60 cm) circular for borders and collar; spare 24" (60 cm) circular in any size smaller than size 7 (4.5 mm).

NOTIONS

Split ring markers or coilless pins; zipper or clasps; tapestry needle; stitch holders; about 80 yards (73 meters) of worsted-weight waste cotton for temporary borders. (White or cream is recommended.) If using a color, test it in hot water to be certain it is colorfast.

GAUGE

Unfelted *14 sts and 21 rows = 4" (10 cm) in Stockinette stitch (St st).*

Felted *About 19 sts and 30 rows = 4" (10 cm). Gauge will vary with the amount of felting.*

FELTING

Because of its size, this vest must be felted more slowly than a small project and requires special handling. Be sure to place vest in a large mesh bag or a zippered pillow protector.

Set washer for a full load, hot water, and delicate cycle. Add a small amount (about 1 tablespoon) of a no-rinse woolwash such as Woolmix or a mild detergent. Reset the washer cycle to agitate longer if necessary. Do not let it drain and spin as this may set a permanent crease in the felt.

Remove vest from the bag every 5 minutes and examine. Watch for places that may be felting more slowly, and speed them up with some hand felting (see notes for hand felting on page 13) before returning the vest to the washer. As vest nears desired size, begin checking more frequently.

When correct size is reached, remove from washer. If detergent was used, rinse thoroughly by hand, not in the machine. Machine rinsing will cause further shrinkage. Use towels to remove as much water from the vest as possible.

Remove the basting, but do not remove cotton borders. Lay vest on a flat surface and pull into shape, checking measurements. You may need to stretch the vest along its width, especially at the center back which tends to shrink more than the other parts. Allow vest to dry completely, away from heat and sunlight. This may take a day or two.

on hold, bind off next 15 (17, 19) sts for underarm, purl 78 (90, 102) sts and place on hold for back, bind off next 15 (17, 19) sts for underarm, P37 (43, 49) sts to end for right front. Important: In each of the 3 sections, mark a st near the center of this row with a pin.

Right Front

(RS) Working on 37 (43, 49) right front sts only, decrease 1 st every other row at armhole edge 5 (6, 7) times as follows: knit to last 3 sts, k2tog, k1—32 (37, 42) sts remain. Work even in St st until there are 56 (64, 66) rows above the pin marking the underarm row, ending with a WS row.

Shape Neck

(RS) Bind off 2 (3, 4) sts at neck edge every other row 3 times—26 (28, 30) sts remain. Then decrease 1 st every other row at neck edge 6 times as follows: k1, ssk, knit to end—20 (22, 24) sts remain. Work even for 4 (6, 6) rows, ending with a RS row—77 (87, 89) rows above underarm marker.

Shape Shoulder

(WS) At shoulder edge, bind off 6 (7, 8) sts every other row twice, then remaining 8 sts. Cut yarn and fasten off.

Left Front

With WS facing, join yarn to left front at center front edge. Purl 1 row. Decrease 1 st every other row at armhole edge 5 (6, 7) times as follows: k1, ssk, knit to end of row—32 (37, 42) sts remain. Work even in St st until there are 56 (64, 66) rows above the pin marking the underarm row, ending with a RS row.

Shape Neck

(WS) Bind off 2 (3, 4) sts at neck edge every other row 3 times—26 (28, 30) sts remain. Then decrease 1 st every other row at neck edge 6 times as follows: p1, p2tog, purl to end—20 (22, 24) sts remain. Work even for 4 (6, 6) rows—77 (87, 89) rows above underarm marker.

Shape shoulder

(RS) At shoulder edge, bind off 6 (7, 8) sts every other row twice, then remaining 8 sts. Cut yarn and fasten off.

Back

With RS facing, join yarn to back section. Decrease 1 st each edge every other row 5 (6, 7) times as follows: k1, ssk, knit to last 3 sts, k2tog, k1—68 (78, 88) sts remain. Work even in St st until there are 76 (86, 88) rows above the pin marking the underarm row. ***Divide for neck:*** (RS) K21 (23, 25), bind off the next 26 (32, 38) sts, knit to end.

Shape shoulders

Work each shoulder separately beginning with left shoulder where yarn is attached.
Rows 1 and 3: (WS) Bind off 6 (7, 8) sts, purl to end.
Row 2: K1, ssk, knit to end.
Row 4: Knit. Turn and bind off remaining 8 sts. Cut yarn and fasten off.
With RS facing, join yarn to right shoulder.
Rows 1 and 3: (RS) Bind off 6 (7, 8) sts, knit to end.
Row 2: P1, p2tog, purl to end.
Row 4: Purl. Turn and bind off remaining 8 sts. Cut yarn and fasten off.

Prepare For Felting

Sew shoulder seams working a flat seam (see Techniques, page 103). Weave in loose ends carefully on WS. ***Temporary Borders:*** This very important step insures that the edges of the vest felt to the proper length. Follow stitch counts carefully. Borders will be considerably shorter than the unfelted vest, causing it to gather. Use the size 7 needle and smooth, worsted-weight cotton for all temporary borders. ***Fronts:*** With RS facing, pick up and knit 83 (92, 97) sts along one front edge, having the bottom st even with the cast-on edge. Purl 1 row, knit 1 row, then bind off knitwise. Repeat on other front edge. ***Neck Edge:*** With RS facing, pick up and knit 71 (81, 89) sts around neck edge, having the first and last sts in the same place as the top front border sts. Purl 1 row, knit 1 row, then bind off knitwise.

Armhole Openings: With RS facing, pick up and knit 92 (104, 108) sts around sleeve opening. Knit 2 rnds then bind off. Baste center front and sleeve openings closed, working through the cotton, not the wool. Tie off and trim any long cotton yarn ends. Follow special felting instructions for vests on page 62. After the vest is felted and completely dry it is ready for knit borders and a collar.

Borders

Do not remove cotton yarn until the correct number of border sts have been picked up. ***Armhole Borders:*** Attach contrast yarn to center of one underarm and with size 7 circular needle, pick up and knit 1 st at the base of each cotton around stitch sleeve opening—92 (104, 108) sts. Cut and remove cotton yarn. Working in rounds, purl 6 rnds of border. With WS facing and using spare, smaller circular needle, pick up the back loops of the first border rnd (these are the loops of contrast color laying directly on the felt), 1 loop for every st. Fold border sts in half with the purl side out, and holding both needles in your left hand, work a 3-needle bind-off (see Techniques, page 103). Cut yarn and fasten off. Repeat for second armhole border. ***Front Borders:*** With contrast yarn and size 7 needles, pick up and knit 1 st at the base of each cotton st on one side of front—83, (92, 97) sts). Cut and remove cotton. Beginning with a knit row, work 6 rows in Reverse St st (knit on WS, purl on RS). Using a spare, smaller circular needle, pick up the back loops of the first border rnd, fold border, and work a 3-needle bind-off as for the armhole borders. Repeat for second front border.

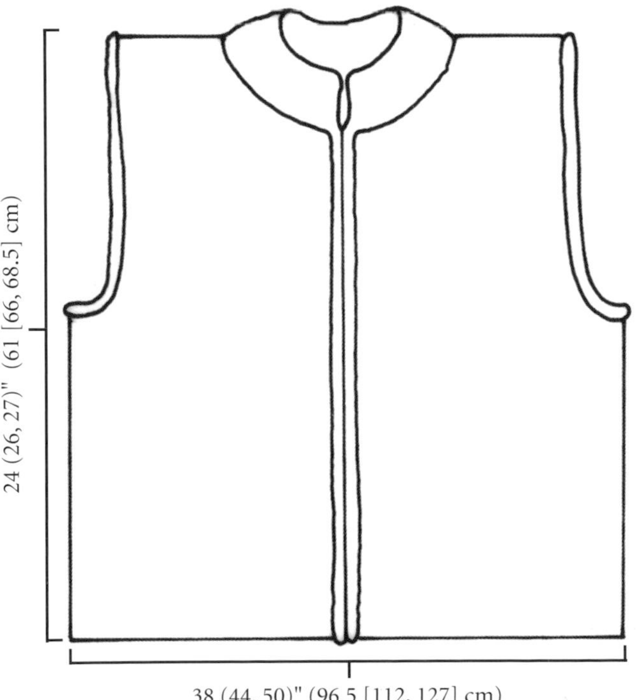

Collar: With contrast yarn and size 7 needles, pick up and knit 3 sts from the top of the right front band, then 1 stitch at the base of each cotton stitch around neck edge, and then 3 sts from the top of the left front band—77 (87, 95 sts). Cut and remove cotton. Begin working in short rows (see Techniques, page 103) as follows:

Row 1: *P1, k1; repeat from * until 55 (65, 73) sts have been worked ending with a p1, wrap next st and turn (W&T), leaving 22 sts unworked at end of row.

Row 2: *K1, p1; repeat from * until 33 (43, 51) sts have been worked ending with a k1, W&T, leaving 22 sts unworked at end of row.

Row 3: Beginning with a p1, work in ribbing as established for 39 (49, 57) sts, W&T.

Row 4: Beginning with a k1, rib 45 (55, 63) sts, W&T.

Row 5: Rib 51 (61, 69) sts, W&T.

Row 6: Rib 57 (67, 75) sts, W&T.

Row 7: Rib 63 (73, 81) sts, W&T.

Row 8: Rib 69 (79, 87) sts, W&T.

Row 9: Rib to end of row.

Work 14 rows even in rib, then repeat Rows 1–9. Work 1 complete row in ribbing. Pick up the back loops of the first border rnd, fold collar, and work a 3-needle bind-off as for the armhole borders.

Finishing

Weave in loose ends on WS. Sew in zipper (see Techniques, page 103) or attach clasps if desired. Steam vest on WS to smooth felt if needed.

warm feet

What could be more comfortable than slipping your feet into a pair of warm, woolly, felted slippers in the morning, or any other time of day? Wool slippers keep your feet dry and comfortable; felting makes them durable and longwearing. For even more cushiony comfort, all of these slippers (except the baby booties) have a double-thick sole.

slippers

SPECIAL FELTING CONSIDERATIONS FOR SLIPPERS

For best results, always felt both slippers of a pair at the same time. Since these slippers are intended to be felted firmly, they'll need extra time in the washing machine to reach their proper size. Even though felting takes longer with slippers, it is very important to check them regularly during agitation. Always remove both slippers from the bag and pull them into shape to check the size.

When you think they've reached the correct size, remove them from washer and rinse under cold, running water. Pull them into shape, and make sure they are both the same length. Put them on occasionally while they are drying to insure a custom fit.

SLIPPERS ARE SLIPPERY!

Felted slippers can be dangerously slippery on some floor surfaces. If your slippers will be worn on floors without carpeting, consider adding suede soles or two-piece slipper bottoms for safety.

Mohair Ballet Slippers

These warm, comfy, and pretty slippers will make you want to give up your street shoes!

Inner sole

Beginning at center of inner sole with circular needle and a double strand of plain wool, loosely cast on (35, 41, 43) [47, 53, 59] sts. *Do not join.* Sole is worked back and forth in garter stitch (knit every row).

Mark the (18th, 21st, 22nd)[24th, 27th, 30th] stitch with a pin or split marker. This is the center toe stitch. To help keep your place, this stitch is shown in italics on all increase and decrease rows and rounds. Knit 1 row. Work short rows (see Techniques, page 103) as follows:

1st Short-row: K1, M1 (see Techniques, page 103), k(16, 19, 20)[22, 25, 28], M1, *k1*, M1, k(12, 15, 16)[17, 20, 22], wrap next st and turn (W&T), k(27, 33, 35)[37, 43, 47], W&T, k(11, 14, 15)[16, 19, 21], M1, k2, M1, *k1*, M1, k2, M1, k(15, 18, 19)[21, 24, 27], M1, k1—(43, 49, 51)[55, 61, 67] sts.

For Women's sizes only:
Next row: Knit.
For Child's sizes S and M only:
Next row: K1, M1, k(18, 21), M1, k2, M1, *k1*, M1, k2, M1, k(18, 21), M1, k1—(49, 55) sts.
For Child's size L and Women's sizes only:
2nd Short-row: K1, M1, k(22)[24, 27, 30], M1, k2, M1, *k1*, M1, k2, M1, k(11)[13, 15, 17], W&T, k (31)

SIZE

Child's sizes are given first; women's sizes follow in [ ]. If there is only one figure or set of instructions, it applies to all sizes. ***Child's*** *(small, medium, large); to fit shoe size up to about (8, 11½, 12).* ***Women's*** *[small, medium, large]; to fit shoe size up to about [6, 8, 10]. Actual size is achieved during felting so you can customize the fit. For in-between sizes, choose the larger size and felt down for firm, long-wearing slippers. For wide feet, add an extra plain knit row between the shaping rows of the sole. For a child with narrow feet too long for the child's large, make a woman's small and omit the knit row after the first short row of sole. Note that adding or subtracting a row on the sole will also increase or decrease the length slightly.*

YARN

(200, 220, 275)[330, 360, 400] yards (183, 201, 251.5)[302, 329, 366] meters of worsted-weight wool and (45, 50, 60)[70, 75, 85] yards (41, 46, 55)[64, 69, 78] meters of worsted-weight mohair/wool blend. Always test your yarns to be sure that they felt to a nice fabric at the gauge given. Slippers are shown in Brown Sheep Nature Spun worsted (100% wool; 245 yd[224m]/100g): #N48 scarlet, or #N62 amethyst, (1, 1, 2)[2, 2, 2] skeins as the main yarn, and Green Mountain Spinnery Mountain Mohair (70% wool, 30% mohair; 140 yd [128 m]/50 g): #5-L lupin, 1 skein, or Brown Sheep Hand Paint Originals (70% mohair, 30% wool; 88 yd [80.5 m]/ 50 g): # HP40 strawberry patch, 1 skein, as the mohair/wool blend contrast yarn.

NEEDLES

Size 13 (9 mm), (16)[24]" (40 cm)[60 cm] circular needle; spare circular needle of the same length in a smaller size. Adjust needle size if necessary to obtain the correct gauge.

NOTIONS

Markers: Split ring markers or coilless pins; tapestry needle; suede slipper bottoms (optional).

GAUGE

Unfelted Gauge *10 sts and 14 rows = 4" (10 cm) in Stockinette stitch (St st) with 1 strand of wool and 1 strand of mohair held together.*
Felted Gauge *About 12 sts and 24 rows = 4" (10 cm). Gauge will vary with the amount of felting.*

FELTING

Follow basic felting instructions and notes at the beginning of this section.

OPTIONAL FINISHING

When slippers are dry, use a stiff brush to brush up the mohair for a furry look if desired. Sew on suede slipper bottoms.

[35, 39, 43], W&T, k(10)[12, 14, 16], M1, k3, M1, k2, M1, *k1*, M1, k2, M1, k3, M1, k(21)[23, 26, 29], M1, k1—(63)[67, 73, 79] sts.
All sizes, last row of sole: Cut 1 strand of wool and join 1 strand of mohair. Continuing with 1 strand of each yarn held together, knit 1 row even. (Color blips of mohair on the RS will be hidden by the outer sole.)

Upper Part

All sizes: Knit 1 row (RS). Do not turn. Place marker for heel and join into round.
Knit (2, 2, 3)[4, 4, 5] rounds even.

Shape Toe

Note: This first round includes a number of turns to shape the toe. Work to where your size ends at the heel marker, then continue with round 2.
Rnd 1: K(22, 25, 29)[31, 34, 37], k2tog, *k1*, ssk, k4, turn, slip 1, p10, turn.
For Child's size S only: Slip 1, k2, k2tog, *k1*, ssk, k2, ssk, knit to end of rnd—44 sts remain.
For Child's size M, L, and Women's sizes only: Slip 1, k2, k2tog, *k1*, ssk, k2, ssk, k3, turn, slip 1, p10, p2tog, p3, turn.
For Child's size M only: Slip 1, k4, k2tog, *k1*, ssk, k4, ssk, knit to end of rnd—46 sts remain.
For Child's size L and Women's sizes only: Slip 1, k4, k2tog, *k1*, ssk, k4, ssk, k2, turn, slip 1, p13, p2tog, p2, turn.
For Child's size L and Women's size S only: Slip 1, k5, k2tog, *k1*, ssk, k5, ssk, knit to end of rnd—50 [54] sts remain.
For Women's sizes M and L only: Slip 1, k5, k2tog, *k1*, ssk, k5, ssk, k2, turn, slip 1, p15, p2tog, p2, turn.
For Women's size M only: Slip 1, k6, k2tog, *k1*, ssk, k6, ssk, knit to end of rnd—56 sts remain.
For Women's size L only: Slip 1, k6, k2tog, *k1*, ssk, k6, ssk, k2, turn, slip 1, p17, p2tog, p2, turn, slip 1, k7, k2tog, *k1*, ssk, k7, ssk, knit to end of rnd—58 sts remain.
All sizes:
Rnd 2: K(17, 16, 17)[19], k2tog, knit to end of rnd—(43, 45, 49)[53, 55, 57] sts remain.
Rnd 3: K(15, 16, 18)[19, 20, 21], k2tog, k(2)[3], k2tog, *k1*, ssk, k(2)[3], ssk, k(15, 16, 18)[19, 20, 21]—(39, 41, 45)[49, 51, 53] sts remain.
Rnd 4: Knit.
Rnd 5: K(14, 15, 17)[18, 19, 20], k2tog, k(1)[2], k2tog, *k1*, ssk, k(1)[2], ssk, k(14, 15, 17)[18, 19, 20]—(35, 37, 41)[45, 47, 49] sts remain.

Cuff

Cut mohair and continue with a single strand of wool. Knit 1 rnd. Purl 3 rnds. With spare circular needle, on inside of slipper, pick up the lower loop of each stitch from ridge of first cuff rnd (the first rnd worked with 1 strand of wool)—(35, 37, 41)[45, 47, 49] loops on spare needle. Fold cuff down to inside and work a 3-needle bind-off (see Techniques, page 103). Cut yarn and fasten off last stitch.

Outer Sole

With a double strand of plain wool and circular needle, cast on (35, 41, 43)[47, 53, 59] sts. Follow instructions for inner sole in your size up to, but not including, the last plain knit row—(49, 55, 63)[67, 73, 79] sts. Do not cut yarn.

Finishing

Sew center seams of inner sole and outer sole. With spare circular needle, RS facing, and beginning at heel, pick up the top loops of the last garter stitch ridge (the plain wool loops) around the outer edge of inner sole-(49, 55, 63)[67, 73, 79] sts. Place outer sole over inner sole and hold both needles in your left hand. With outer sole facing and continuing with double strand of wool, work a 3-needle bind-off all the way around the sole.

With a single strand of wool, tack the 2 soles together down the center, using very loose, short, backstitches. Weave in loose ends on WS. Check for holes and darn if needed.

Felted Moccasins

Felted firmly and finished with leather lacing and leather soles, these felted moccasins look like the real thing.

Prepare Temporary Ties

Needed if leather ties will be added; make 2.

Using worsted-weight waste cotton, cut four lengths at least 1 [1½] yd (1 [1.25] m) long. Hold these strands together and fold in half so there are 8 strands with a fold at one end. Set aside.

Vamp (top inset)

With circular needle and a double strand of yarn, cast on (3)[5] sts. Working back and forth in rows of garter stitch, knit 2 rows even.

1st Inc row: K1, M1 (see Techniques, page 103), k(1)[3], M1, k1—(5)[7] sts.

Knit (5)[7] rows even.

2nd Inc row: K1, M1, k(3)[5], M1, k1—(7)[9] sts.

Knit (5)[7] rows even.

3rd Inc row: K1, M1, k(5)[7], M1, k1—(9)[11] sts.

Knit (1, 3, 5)[5, 7, 9] rows even.

For Child's L and Men's sizes only:

4th Inc row: K1, M1, k(7)[9], M1, k1—(11)[13] sts.

For Child's L and Men's sizes only: Knit (1)[5, 7, 9] rows even.

All sizes: Work short rows (see Techniques, page 103) as follows: K(6, 6, 8)[9], wrap next st and turn (W&T), k(3, 3, 5)[5], W&T, k(4, 4, 6)[6], W&T, k(5, 5, 7)[7], W&T, k(7, 7, 9)[8];

End Men's sizes only: W&T, k9, W&T, k11.

All sizes:

Last increase row: K(4, 4, 5)[6], M1, k1, M1, k(4, 4, 5)[6]—(11, 11, 13)[15] sts. Bind off sts loosely knitwise. Cut yarn.

With spare circular needle, pick up (21, 23, 27)[37, 41, 45] sts around outer edge of vamp.

SIZE

Child's sizes are given first; men's sizes follow in [ ]. If there is only one figure or set of instructions, it applies to all sizes. ***Child's*** *(small, medium, large); to fit shoe size up to about (10, 13, 3).* ***Men's*** *[small, medium, large]; to fit shoe size up to about [9, 11, 13]. Actual size is achieved during felting so you can customize the fit. For in-between sizes, choose the larger size and felt down for firm, long-wearing slippers. For a man with narrow feet, omit the knit row after first short-row of sole. This will also shorten the slipper slightly.*

YARN

(250, 280, 350)[650, 700, 750] yards (229, 256, 320)[594, 640, 689] meters of heavy worsted-weight wool. Always test your yarns to be sure that they felt to a nice fabric at the gauge given. The slippers pictured were made in Baabajoes 10-ply Woolpak (100% wool; 430yd [393m]/250g): #27 goldstone and #28 brownstone, (1) [2] hanks.

NEEDLES

Size 13 (9 mm), (16")[24"] (40 cm)[60 cm] circular; spare circular of the same length in a smaller size. Adjust needle size if necessary to obtain the correct gauge.

NOTIONS

Markers: Split ring markers or coilless pins; tapestry needle; optional: leather lacing; suede slipper soles or 2-piece slipper bottoms.

GAUGE

Unfelted Gauge *9 sts and 13 rows = 4"(10 cm) in Stockinette stitch (St st) with 2 strands of wool held together.*
Felted Gauge *About 11.5 sts and 24 rows = 4" (10 cm). Gauge will vary with the amount of felting.*

FELTING

Follow basic felting instructions and notes at the beginning of this section. It is very important to keep the temporary cotton ties loose by pulling on them every time you check the felting progress. If the wool felts around the tie, it can be impossible to get it loose again.

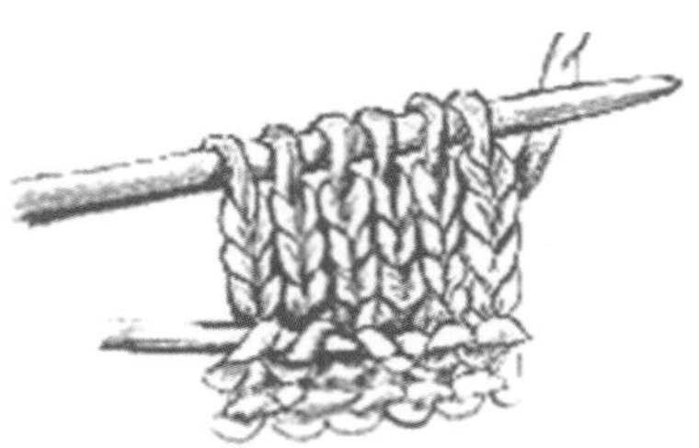

Note: Pick up sts by slipping needle through outer edge of each ridge and cast on st.

Set this piece aside and begin inner sole.

Inner Sole

With circular needle and a double strand of yarn, loosely cast on (35, 41, 43)[53, 59, 65] sts. *Do not join.* Sole is worked back and forth in garter stitch (knit every row). Mark (18th, 21st, 22nd)[27th, 30th, 33rd] stitch with a pin or split marker. This is the center toe stitch. To help keep your place, this stitch is shown in italics on all increase and decrease rows and rounds.
Knit 1 row. Work short rows (see Techniques, page 103) as follows:
1st Short-row: K1, M1, k(16, 19, 20)[25, 28, 31], M1, *k1*, M1, k(12, 15, 16)[19, 22, 25], W&T, k(27, 33, 35)[41, 47, 53], W&T, k(11, 14, 15)[18, 21, 24], M1, k2, M1, *k1*, M1, k2, M1, k(15, 18, 19)[24, 27, 30], M1, k1—(43, 49, 51)[61, 67, 73] sts.
Men's sizes only: Knit 1 row.
For Child's sizes S and M only:
Next row: K1, M1, k(18, 21), M1, k2, M1, *k1*, M1, k2, M1, k(18, 21), M1, k1—(49, 55) sts.
For Child's size L and Men's sizes only:
2nd Short-row: K1, M1, k(22)[27, 30, 33], M1, k2, M1, *k1*, M1, k2, M1, k(11)[13, 16, 19], W&T, k(31)[35, 41, 47], W&T, k(10)[12, 15, 18], M1, k3, M1, k2, M1, *k1*, M1, k2, M1, k3, M1, k(21)[26, 29, 32], M1, k1—(63)[73, 79, 85] sts.
For Men's sizes only: Knit 1 row.
For Men's sizes only:
Next row: [K1, M1] twice, k[28, 31, 34], [M1, k2] 3 times, M1, *k1*, M1, [k2, M1] 3 times, k[28, 31, 34], [M1, k1] twice—[85, 91, 97] sts.

All sizes, last row of sole: Knit 1 row even.

Upper Part

All Sizes: Knit 1 row (RS). *Do not turn.* Place marker for heel and join into round.
Knit (1, 1, 2)[3] rnds even.

Heel Shaping

Note: Each of the following 2 [3] rows begins and ends at the heel marker and has two turns.

1st Shaping row: K(13, 15, 17)[25, 27, 29], turn, slip 1, p(25, 29, 33)[49, 53, 57], turn, slip 1, k(12, 14, 16)[24, 26, 28], ending at heel marker.
2nd Shaping row: K(6, 7, 8)[18, 20, 22], turn, slip 1, p(11, 13, 15)[35, 39, 43], turn, slip 1, k(5, 6, 7)[17, 19, 21], ending at heel marker.
For Men's sizes only:
3rd Shaping row: K[11, 13, 15], turn, slip 1, p[21, 25, 29], turn, slip 1, [k10, 12, 14], ending at heel marker.
Decrease Rnd—work as follows:
Children's sizes:
K(5, 6, 7), ssk, k(5, 6, 7), ssk, k(2, 3, 2,), k2tog, *k1, k2tog; repeat from * (1, 1, 2) more times, *k1*, ssk, *k1, ssk; repeat from * (1, 1, 2) more times, k(2, 3, 2), *k2tog, k(5, 6, 7); repeat from * once more—(39, 45, 51) sts.
Men's sizes:
K(10, 12, 14), ssk, *k5, ssk; repeat from * 1 more time, k(2, 3, 4), k2tog, *k2, k2tog; repeat from * 2 more times, *k1*, ssk, *k2, ssk; repeat from * 2 more times, k[2, 3, 4], *k2tog, k5; repeat from * once more, k2tog, k[10, 12, 14]—[71, 77, 83] sts.
Cut yarn. Leaving marker in place, slip last (9, 11, 12)[17, 18, 19] sts just worked back onto left needle. Turn work so that inside is facing.

Join Vamp

Note: Vamp has no RS or WS.

Place vamp over inside of moccasin and hold both needles in your left hand. With vamp facing and using double strand of yarn, work a 3-needle join (see Techniques, page 103) by knitting together a stitch from vamp (front needle) with a stitch from moccasin (back needle). Continue in this manner until all (21, 23, 27)[37, 41, 45] vamp sts have been worked off spare needle. Set this needle aside and k(9, 11, 12)[17, 18, 19] sts, ending at heel marker.

Note: You will be working with inside of slipper facing.

Next rnd: K(8, 10, 11)[16, 17, 18], k2tog, k(7, 8, 10)[13, 15, 17], *M1, k2; repeat from * (0)[1] more time, M1, *k1*, *M1, k2; repeat from * (0)[1] more time, M1, k(7, 8, 10)[13, 15, 17], k2tog, k(8, 10, 11)[16, 17, 18].
Next rnd: K(9, 11, 12)[17, 18, 19], loosely bind off next (23, 25, 29)[41, 45, 49] sts, k(9, 11, 12)[17, 18, 19], ending at heel marker, remove marker, knit next (9, 11, 12)[17, 18, 19] sts, turn. (See Mid-row BO, Techniques, page 103.)

Cuff

worked back and forth in rows
Row 1: Purl.
Row 2: Knit.
With spare circular needle, on the inside of moccasin pick up the top loop of each stitch from last purl ridge before cuff (see illustration on page 73)—(18, 22, 24)[34, 36, 38] loops on spare needle.

Place the 8 strands of waste cotton between the 2 needles and fold working needle down to meet spare needle. The cotton should be encased in the cuff between the needles. Holding both needles in your left hand, work a 3-needle bind off (see Techniques, page 103). Cut yarn and fasten off last stitch.

Sew the inside of the cuff end to the first 2 bound off sts of the vamp top, being careful not to catch the cotton or close up the opening in the end of cuff. The opening should be on the outside of the vamp. Repeat on other side of moccasin.

Outer Sole

With double strand of wool and circular needle, cast on (35, 41, 43)[53, 59, 65] sts and follow instructions for inner sole in your size up to, but not including, the last plain knit row. Do not cut yarn.

Finishing

Sew center seams of inner and outer sole. With spare circular needle, RS facing, and beginning at heel, pick up the top loop of the last garter stitch ridge around the outer edge of inner sole—(49, 55, 63)[85, 91, 97] sts. Place outer sole over inner sole and hold both needles in your left hand. With outer sole facing and continuing with double strand of wool, work a 3-needle bind off. With a single strand of wool, tack the 2 soles together down the center, using very loose, short backstitches. Weave in loose ends on WS. Check for holes and darn if needed. Tie cut ends of cotton through the fold end. Trim excess from the cut end, but do not cut the fold. It will be used later to pull the ties through the cuff. *Important:* Keep the cotton loose in the casing during felting by pulling on it every time you do a progress check.

Optional Finishing

To add leather ties, when slippers are felted and dry, cut the knot in the waste cotton without cutting the loop end. Loop the leather tie through the folded end of the cotton and pull it through the cuff. Make holes with a knitting needle to lace the ends of the tie through the top of the vamp. Sew on suede soles, or slipper bottoms if desired. For an authentic moccasin look, add leather lacing around the vamp.

Baby Booties

Well-dressed babies all want felted booties! For a touch of luxury, use an angora yarn for the contrast color.

With MC loosely cast on 30 (34) sts.
Row 1: Knit.
Row 2: (RS) K1, M1 (see Techniques, page 103), k13 (15), M1, k2, M1, k13 (15), M1, k1—34 (38) sts.
Row 3: K26 (30), wrap next st and turn (W&T) (see Techniques, page 103), k8 (10), M1, k2, M1, k8 (10), W&T, k28 (32)—36 (40) sts.
Row 4: K1, M1, k16 (18), M1, k2, M1, k16 (18), M1, k1—40 (44).
Row 5: Knit.
Row 6: K1, M1, k16 (18), [M1, k2] 3 times, M1, k16 (18), M1, k1—46 (50) sts.
Knit 5 rows even.

Shape Instep

Row 1: (RS) K16 (17), ssk, k10 (12), k2tog, k16 (17)—44 (48) sts.
Row 2: and all even numbered rows through row 12 (14): Knit.
Row 3: K16 (17), ssk, k8 (10), k2tog, k16 (17)—42 (46) sts.
Row 5: K16 (17), ssk, k6 (8), k2tog, k16 (17)—40 (44) sts.
Row 7: K16 (17), ssk, k4 (6), k2tog, k16 (17)—38 (42) sts.
Row 9: K16 (17), ssk, k2 (4), k2tog, k16 (17)—36 (40) sts.
For size L only:
Row 11: K17, ssk, k2, k2tog, k17—38 sts.
All sizes:
Row 11 (13): K12 (13), ssk, k1, ssk, k2, k2tog, k1, k2tog, k12 (13)—32 (34) sts.
Size S only:
Row 13: (Eyelet row) K2tog, *yo, k2tog, k2tog; repeat from * to last 2 sts, yo, k2tog—24 sts.
Size S only:
Row 14: (WS) K1, *(k1, p1) in the yo , k2; repeat from * ending last repeat k1—32 sts.

SIZE

Small (large); to fit about 3 (6) months. Exact size is determined by felting time.

YARN

95 (105) yards (87 [96] meters) of main color (MC) and 16–17 yards (15–15.5 meters) of contrast color (CC) in a light worsted or DK-weight yarn. Always test your yarns to be sure that they felt to a nice fabric at the gauge given. The booties pictured were made in Bryspun kid-n-ewe (50% wool/50% mohair; 120 yd [110m]/50g): color 430 (MC), with color 500 (CC), 1 skein each; and kid-n-ewe color 320 (MC), with Anny Blatt Angora Super (70% angora, 30% wool; 116 yd [106 m]/25 g): fuchsia, 1 skein each.

NEEDLES

Size 10 (6 mm) straight needles; a spare needle size 8 (5 mm) or smaller. Adjust needle size if necessary to obtain the correct gauge.

NOTIONS

Tapestry needle; small amount of worsted-weight, waste cotton yarn for temporary lacing.

GAUGE

Unfelted Gauge *14 sts and 28 rows = 4" (10 cm) in garter stitch.*
Felted Gauge *About 18 sts and 34 rows = 4" (10 cm). Gauge will vary with the amount of felting.*

FELTING

Small items like these booties may take longer to felt than larger items. It is helpful to turn them inside out every other time you do a progress check and it is especially important to add something to the washer to increase agitation.

SPECIAL NOTE

If these booties are worn by a child ready to stand or walk, they will need a non-slip sole. Fabric stores sell a material for pajama feet that can be cut and sewn on to the bottoms of the booties.

Size L only:
Row 15: (Eyelet row) K2tog, [yo, k2tog, k2tog] 3 times, yo, k2tog, k2, k2tog, [yo, k2tog, k2tog] 3 times, yo, k2tog—26 sts.
Size L only:
Row 16: (WS) K1, [(k1, p1) in the yo, k2] 4 times, k2, [(k1, p1) in the yo, k2] 4 times, ending last repeat k1—34 sts.
All Sizes: Knit 2 rows even.

Bootie Top

Work each side of bootie top separately, beginning with the side that the yarn is attached to. Work short rows (see Techniques, page 103) as follows:

First Side

Row 1: (RS) K16 (17), turn, leaving remaining stitches unworked.
Row 2: K16 (17).
Row 3: K12 (13), W&T, k12 (13).
Row 4: K8 (9), W&T, k8 (9).
Row 5: K4 (5), W&T, k4 (5).
Row 6: K16 (17). Cut yarn.

Second Side

With RS facing, rejoin yarn at center front.
Row 1: (RS) K16 (17).
Row 2: K12 (13), W&T, k12 (13).
Row 3: K8 (9), W&T, k8 (9).
Row 4: K4 (5), W&T, k4 (5).
Rows 5 and 6: K16 (17). Cut yarn after Row 6.

With wrong side facing join CC at back seam edge.
Row 1: K16 (17), pick up and knit 4 sts across center front, k16 (17)—36 (38) sts.
Row 2: Knit.
Row 3: Purl.
Row 4: Knit.
With RS facing and spare smaller needle, pick up the lower loops of the first row of CC. Fold working needle down to meet the spare needle. Holding both needles in your left hand, work a 3-needle bind off (see Techniques, page 103).

Finishing

Sew center back and sole seam with a loose overcast stitch. Weave in loose ends on WS. Check for holes and darn if needed. Run cotton waste yarn through eyelets and tie. When felted and dry, remove cotton and add ribbon or cord ties.

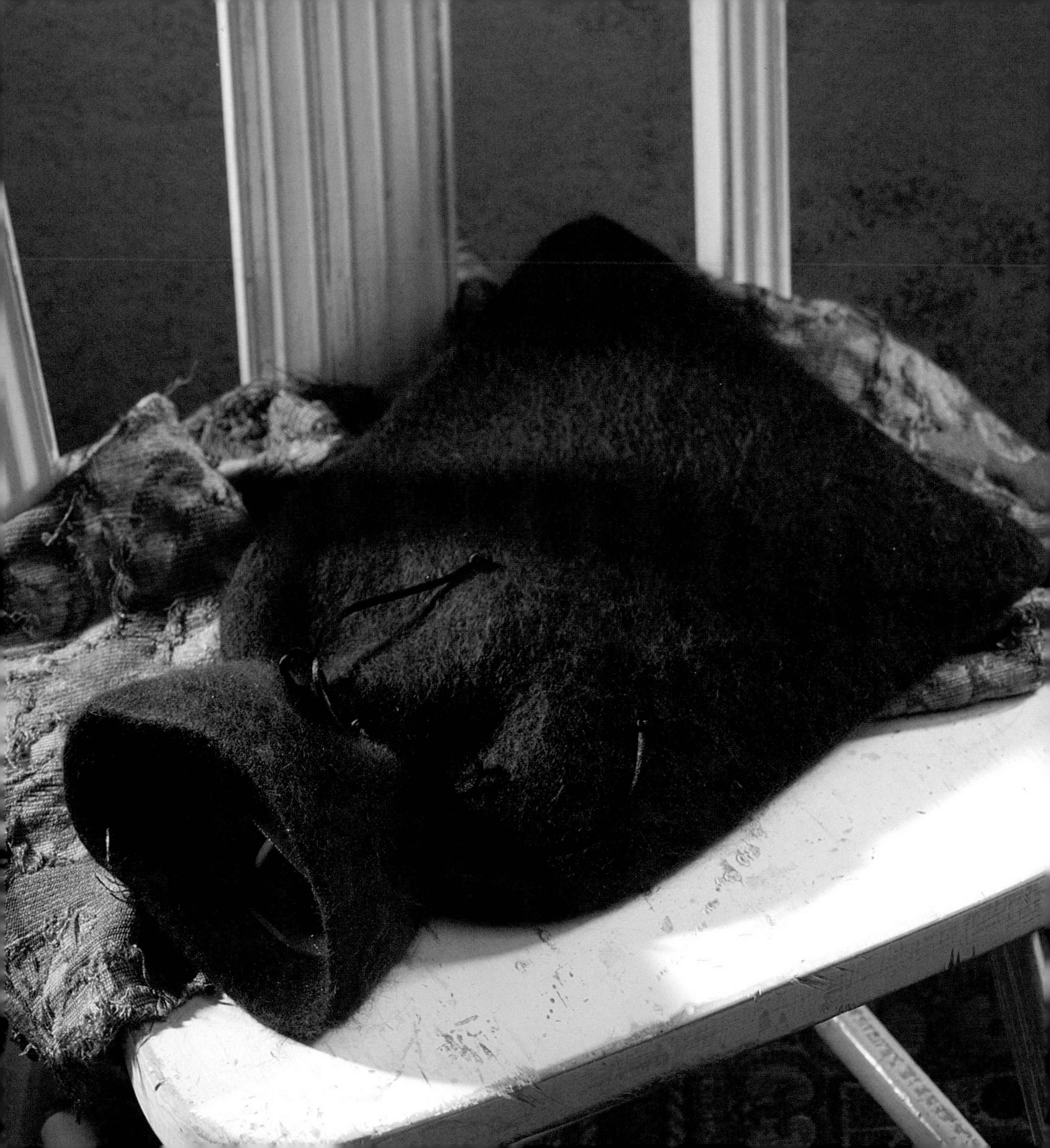

comforts of home

Felted knits add the warm touch of wool throughout your home! In this chapter you will find something for almost every room in your house. Make a rug and pillows for the den; a tea cozy, oven mitt and trivets for the kitchen; pretty things for your bedroom dresser; and even a cover for your hot water bottle so it can be left in any room of your house.

Felted Rug

A small felted rug knit in garter stitch using thick wool is sure to look good by the hearth. Once felted, the garter ridges are still visible and add an interesting texture to the fabric.

Note: To keep a clean break between colors, always change them on the same side of the work. The rug is shown with color changes on the right side (RS). The opposite side has more blended colors. If you prefer this as your RS, knit up the borders from that side and work the yarn ends in on the other side.

With MC, loosely cast on 49 sts. *Do not join.* Working back and forth in rows of garter st (knit every row), knit 5 rows.
Inc row: K3, *inc in next st, k5; repeat from * to last 4 sts, inc in next st, k3—57 sts.
Knit 11 more rows in MC.
Begin Stripe Pattern: Knit 2 rows with A, 2 rows B, 2 rows A, 20 rows MC.
Repeat 26 row stripe pattern 3 more times.
Knit 2 rows with A, 2 rows B, 2 rows A, 12 rows MC.
Dec row: K3, *k2tog, k5; repeat from * to last 5 sts, k2tog, k3—49 sts.
Knit 4 more rows with MC.
Bind off loosely knitwise. Cut yarn and fasten off.

Side Borders

With RS facing, pick up and knit 73 sts along one side edge (1 st for every garter-stitch ridge).
Turn and bind off loosely knitwise. Cut yarn and fasten off. Repeat on the other side edge.

Finishing

Weave in loose ends on WS.

SIZES

24" by 34" (61 by 86 cm). Other sizes may be made by adjusting stitch and row count, but it is difficult to felt a rug much larger than this in a home washing machine.

YARN

Total of 510 yards (466.5 meters) of super-bulky-weight yarn. The stripe pattern shown requires about 400 yards (366 meters) of super-bulky-weight yarn in main color (MC), 130 yards (119 meters) of color (A) and 70 yards (64 meters) of color (B) in bulky-weight yarn. Note: Yardage for colors A and B allow you to use a double strand of bulky-weight yarn for the stripes. Always test your yarns to be sure that they felt to a nice fabric at the gauge given. The rug is shown in Brown Sheep Burley Spun (100% wool; 130 yd [119 m]/ 8 oz): #181 prairie fire (MC), 4 skeins. Stripes are knit with a double strand of Brown Sheep Lamb's Pride Bulky (85% wool, 15% mohair; 125 yd [114.5 m]/ 4 oz): #M-08 wild oak (A), 1 skein, and Mountain Colors 3-ply Montana Wool (100% wool; 150 yd [137 m]/4 oz): northern lights (B), 1 skein.

NEEDLES

Size 15 (10 mm), 32"–40" (81.5–101.5 cm) circular. Adjust needle size if necessary to obtain the correct gauge.

NOTIONS

Tapestry needle.

GAUGE

Unfelted *8 sts and 13 rows = 4" (10 cm) in garter st.*
Felted *About 9½ sts and 24 rows = 4" (10 cm).*

FELTING

This rug is a large and heavy piece to felt. Use a medium-to-high water level and once agitation begins, check to be sure that the rug is moving in the water. I put the rug in a large zippered pillow protector, added two pair of jeans to balance the load, and felted until the stitches were tightened, but not firmly felted. Once the rug is felted, pull it into shape, straightening edges as needed, and allow to dry. Use a nonslip pad under the rug on any smooth floor surface.

Pillows

Colorful pillows liven up your home. Made in bulky-weight yarns, they're rugged, long wearing, and knit up quickly. Sachet pillows, made in lighter weight yarn, add a pleasant scent to your drawers and make quick and easy gifts.

Note: When you're picking up and knitting sts along the side edges, work through just one strand at the very end of the garter ridge.

SIZES

Accent pillows: *14" (16") [35.5 (40) cm] square, excluding border.*

Sachet Pillows: *4½" (11.5 cm) square. Accent pillow sizes are listed first in ( ); sachet pillow size follows in [ ]. If there is only one figure or set of instructions, it applies to all sizes.*

YARN

Accent pillows: *330 (430) yards (302 [393] meters) of bulky-weight yarn.* ***Sachet Pillows:*** *60 yards (55 meters) main color (MC), 15 yards (14 meters) contrast color (CC) of DK- or worsted-weight yarn. Always test your yarns to be sure that they felt to a nice fabric at the gauge given. Note: The coasters on page 88 are a great way to test yarn and gauge for the pillows. Multicolored accent pillow is shown in Mountain Colors 3-ply Montana Wool (100% wool; 150 yd [137 m]/ 4 oz): northern lights, 3 skeins. Solid-color accent pillows are shown in Brown Sheep Lamb's Pride Bulky (85% wool, 15% mohair; 125 yd [114.5 m]/ 4 oz): #M26 medieval red, and #M82 blue flannel, 3 (4) skeins. Both are very solid yarns and felt to a corduroy look when worked in garter stitch. Using a soft-spun yarn will result in a fabric with a smoother finish.*

Sachet pillow is shown in Bryspun kid-n-ewe (50% kid mohair, 50% wool; 120 yd [110 m]/50 g): #430 green, 1 skein, and Mannings Hawthorne Cottage English Leicester DK (100% wool; 189 yd [173 m]/3.5 oz): #32 handpaint, 1 skein.

NEEDLES

For accent pillows: Size 13 (9 mm), 29" (73.5 cm) circular. For sachet pillows: Size 10 (6 mm) 16" (40 cm) circular. You'll also need 2 spare circular needles, the same size or smaller than the main needles. One of the spare needles should be the same length as the working needle or longer. Adjust needle size if necessary to obtain the correct gauge.

NOTIONS

Size K (7 mm) crochet hook; small amount of worsted-weight, waste cotton for provisional (temporary) cast-on; split ring markers or coilless pins; fine crochet cotton thread for basting; pillow form in appropriate size for pillows; small bag of potpourri for sachets; tapestry needle. Optional: 3 to 7 buttons in your choice of sizes and styles for pillows.

GAUGE

Unfelted *10 [12] sts and 20 [24] rows = 4" (10 cm) in garter st.*

Felted *About 12 [17] sts and 24 [34] rows = 4" (10 cm).*

FELTING

Important Note: Before felting, use a fine cotton crochet thread to loosely baste the opening closed. Follow basic felting instructions on page 10 until the measurement inside the border is the desired size. Once felting is complete, pull pillow into shape and check measurements. If necessary, use pins to hold the pillow square while drying.

Front

With crochet hook and waste yarn, chain (42, 50)[20] plus 3 or 4 extra. With working yarn and main circular needle, pick up and knit (42, 50)[20] sts, working through the bumps on the underside of the chain (see Techniques page 00). Work back and forth in garter st (knit every row) for (83, 99)[39] rows, ending ready to begin a RS row—(42, 50)[20] garter ridges on RS. Knit 1 more row, marking the first st as a corner. *Do not turn.* Rotate work so that side edge is at top. Pick up and knit a st from the end of the first garter ridge

and mark as a corner. Continuing across the side edge, pick up and knit 1 st at the end of every ridge—(42, 50)[20] sts on side edge, counting corner st. Cut and remove the waste yarn from cast-on edge, slipping the live sts onto a spare needle—(41, 49)[19] sts, (1 st is lost at the end). Knit the first st and mark as a corner, then continue knitting across, increase 1 st near the end for (42, 50)[20] sts. Rotate work again. Pick up and knit sts along 2nd side, marking first st as corner—(41, 49)[19] sts between each marked corner st and (168, 200) [80] sts total. Cut yarn. Slip the front sts onto a spare circular needle and set aside.

First Half of Back

With working yarn, cast on (32, 38)[15] sts. Knit 2 rows.
Inc row: (WS) K(2, 2)[1], *inc in next st, k2; repeat from * to last (3, 3)[2] sts, inc in next st, k(2, 2)[1]—(42, 50)[20] sts. Work even in garter st for (48, 56)[20] more rows—(26, 30)[12] ridges total on the right side (RS). Slip these sts to a spare needle. Cut yarn and set aside.

Second Half of Back

Work the same as for first half. Do not cut yarn. Knit 1 more row, marking the last st of this row as a corner st. Rotate work so that side edge is at top. Pick up and knit 1 st from each of the first (16, 20)[8] garter ridges. Place the first back piece, RS up, under the piece you are working on, overlapping the pieces by (10, 10)[4] ridges. Pick up the next (10, 10)[4] sts through the edge of both layers, working through 1 strand of each layer. Continue picking up and knitting sts along the side edge of second half, working 1 st at the end of each of the remaining (16, 20)[8] ridges, marking the last st as a corner st. Rotate work and knit the (42, 50)[20] sts off the spare needle, marking the last st as a corner st. Rotate work. Pick up and knit sts along 2nd side, overlapping the back sections to match the opposite side and marking the last st as a corner—(41, 49)[19] sts between each marked corner st and (168, 200)[80] total.

Joining and Border

Lay back piece, RS down, with garter ridges running vertically and needle points at top right corner. Lay pillow top, RS up, over the back, with garter ridges horizontal and needle points at top right corner.
Rnd 1: With RS of pillow top facing, work a 3-needle join (See Techniques, page 103) around the entire pillow, checking that corner sts match.
Rnd 2: *P1, M1 purlwise (see Techniques page 103), p(41, 49)[19], M1 purlwise; repeat from * 3 more times.
Rnd 3: Bind off loosely knitwise, *and at the same time* increase each side of corner sts as follows: *K1, M1, knit to next corner st, M1; repeat from * 3 more times, bind off last st. Cut yarn and fasten off carefully for a smooth corner.

Finishing

Weave in loose ends on WS.
When dry, insert pillow form or, for sachet pillows, insert a muslin bag of potpourri. Secure opening by tacking invisibly with sewing thread and attach buttons if desired.

In the Kitchen

Wool is heat- and water-resistant, which makes it perfect for the kitchen. A tea cozy is perfect for keeping that last cup of tea hot, and you're likely to use the oven mitt, coasters, and trivet on a daily basis. A matching set makes a great gift!

Tea Cozy (see Materials, page 86)

With circular needle and color B, loosely cast on 80 (90) sts. Place marker and join, being careful not to twist sts. Purl 5 rnds. Cut yarn. With spare circular needle, pick up the lower loops of the cast-on edge. Fold the cast-on edge up to the inside like a hem. Join color A and work a 3-needle join (see Techniques, page 103).

Inc rnd: For Size M only: *K7, inc in next st; repeat from *—90 sts.

Inc rnd: For Size L only: *K7, inc in next st, k6, inc in next st; repeat from * around—102 sts.

All sizes: Shaping Rnd: K29 (33), *wrap next st and turn (W&T) (see Techniques, page 103), p13 (15), W&T, k20 (22), W&T, p27 (29), W&T*, k65 (73), repeat between asterisks once more, k37 (40), ending at beginning of rnd marker. Knit 17 (20) rnds in St st (knit every rnd).

Shape Top

Rnd 1: Ssk, k41 (47), k2tog, place marker, ssk, k41 (47), k2tog—86 (98) sts.

Rnd 2: Knit.

Rnd 3: *Ssk, knit to 2 sts before next marker, k2tog; repeat from * once more—82 (94) sts.

Repeat Rnds 2–3 until 66 (74) sts remain. Knit 1 rnd even. Repeat Rnd 3 only until 6 sts remain. Cut yarn and draw tail through remaining sts. Pull together tightly and fasten off.

Top Loop

With 2 dpn and color B, cast on 2 sts and knit 5" (12.5 cm) of I-cord (see Techniques, page 103). Cut yarn and draw tail through 2 sts. Pull together tightly

and fasten off. Sew ends together, then sew loop securely to top of cozy.

Finishing

Weave in loose ends on WS.

Oven Mitt (see Materials, page 86)

With circular needle and color B, loosely cast on 35 sts. Work as for tea cozy through end of 3-needle join, changing to color A before working the join.

Inc rnd: *K6, inc in next st; repeat from * around—40 sts. Knit 18 rnds even.

Thumb Gusset

Rnd 1: K2, M1(see Techniques, page 103), knit to last 2 sts, M1, k2—42 sts.

Rnds 2–6: Knit.

Rnd 7: K4, M1, knit to last 4 sts, M1, k4—44 sts.

Rnds 8–12: Knit.

Rnd 13: K6, M1, knit to last 6 sts, M1, k6—46 sts.

Rnds 14 and 15: Knit.

Divide for Thumb Opening

Knit 1 rnd, ending 7 sts before marker. Slip the next 7 sts onto a holder, remove marker, and slip the next 7 sts onto the holder—32 sts remain on needle, 14 sts on

holder. Replace marker and join the remaining 32 sts into rnd. Knit 10 rnds even.

Shape Top

Rnd 1: *Ssk, k12, k2tog; repeat from * once—28 sts
Rnds 2–7: Knit.
Rnd 8: *Ssk, k10, k2tog; repeat from * once —24 sts
Rnd 9: Knit.
Rnd 10: *Ssk, k8, k2tog; repeat from * once —20 sts
Rnd 11: Knit.
Rnd 12: *Ssk, k6, k2tog; repeat from * once—16 sts.
Rnd 13: *Ssk, k4, k2tog; repeat from * once—12 sts.
Rnd 14: *Ssk, k2, k2tog; repeat from * once—8 sts.
Rnd 15: *Ssk, k2tog; repeat from * once—4 sts.
Cut yarn and draw tail through remaining sts. Pull together tightly and fasten off.

Thumb

Slip the 14 sts from the holder onto dpn. With second dpn, pick up 2 sts from body of mitten. Arrange sts evenly on 3 dpn, place marker between the 2 picked up sts for beginning of rnd and join—16 sts.
Rnds 1–4: Knit.
Rnd 5: Ssk, knit to last 2 sts, k2tog—14 sts.
Rnd 6: Knit.
Rnds 7–10: Repeat rnds 5 and 6 two more times. —10 sts remain.
Rnd 11: *K2tog; repeat from *—5 sts. Cut yarn and

SIZES

Tea Cozy: *Medium (large): 15" (17") wide by 9½" (11") high [38 (43) by 24 (28) cm]. The medium size fits most standard 6-cup teapots; make the large for oversize pots. These measurements will vary with the amount of felting.* ***Oven Mitt:*** *11" by 4½" (28 by 11.5 cm) Cuff measures 6½" (16.5 cm).* ***Trivet:*** *7½" (19 cm) square.* ***Coaster:*** *4" (10 cm) square.*

YARN

Bulky-weight yarn. ***Tea Cozy:*** *150 (200) yards (137 [183] meters) main color (MC) and 30 (35) yards (27.5 [32] meters) contrast color (CC).* ***Oven Mitt:*** *125 yards (114.5 meters) main color (MC) and 15 yards (14 meters) contrast color (CC).* ***Trivet:*** *50 yards (46 meters) main color (MC) and 25 yards (23 meters) contrast color (CC).* ***Coaster:*** *30 yards (27.5 meters). Oven Mitt, Tea Cozy, and Trivet are all shown in Brown Sheep Lamb's Pride Bulky (85% wool, 15% mohair; 125 yd [114.5 m]/ 4 oz): #M29 jacks plum (A) and #M27 ponderosa pine (B). Oven Mitt and Trivet, 1 skein each A and B; Tea Cozy 2 skeins A, 1 skein B. Coasters were made using yarn left over from the accent pillows. (For yarn details see accent pillows.) Always test your yarns to be sure that they felt to a nice fabric at the gauge given.*

NEEDLES

Tea Cozy: *Size 13 (9 mm), 24" (60 cm) circular and 2 double-pointed needles (dpn); spare 24" (60 cm) size 10 or smaller circular needle.* ***Oven Mitt:*** *Size 13 (9 mm): 16" (40 cm) circular and set of 4 double-pointed (dpn); spare 16" (40 cm) size 10 or smaller circular needle.* ***Coaster and Trivet:*** *Size 13 (9 mm), 24" (60 cm) circular for trivet and 16" (40 cm) circular for coaster. Adjust needle size if necessary to obtain the correct gauge.*

NOTIONS

Markers; coilless pins for trivet or coasters; Size K (7 mm) crochet hook to make optional hanging loops on oven mitt or trivet.

GAUGE

Unfelted *11 sts and 15 rows = 4" (10 cm) in Stockinette stitch (St st).*
Felted *About 13 sts and 20 rows = 4" (10 cm). Gauge will vary with the amount of felting.*

FELTING

Follow basic felting instructions on page 10 for all pieces, felting until they are down to the desired size. The oven mitt and trivet are most useful if felted to a very firm fabric.

draw tail through remaining sts. Pull together tightly and fasten off.

Hanging Loop

(optional) With crochet hook and either color, crochet a loose chain 6" (15 cm) long. Cut yarn and fasten off. Fold in half and sew the ends together, then slip st to inside of mitt.

Finishing

Weave in loose ends on WS.

Coaster and Trivet

Coaster size is given first, trivet size follows in [ ]. If there is only one figure or set of instructions, it applies to both.

Note: Stripes can be added to either the coaster or the trivet. For a clean line between colors always change color on a right side (RS) row.

For solid color trivet or coaster: Loosely cast on 12 [23] sts. Work in garter stitch (knit every row) for a total of 23 [45] rows.
For stripe pattern trivet: With color B, loosely cast on 23 sts. Knit 9 rows B, *2 rows A, 10 rows B; repeat from * 2 more times.
For both styles you should end ready to begin a RS row and have 12 [23] ridges of garter stitch on the RS.

Border

Change to color A if desired.
Rnd 1: Knit across the 12 [23] sts, rotate work so that side edge is at top. Pick up and knit 12 [23] sts along this edge (1 st for each ridge), pick up and knit 12 [23] sts from the cast-on edge, then 12 [23] from 2nd side. Mark the last st of each side as a corner stitch with a pin. Join and work border in rounds.
Rnd 1: Purl.
Rnd 2: Bind off very loosely, and *at the same time* increase as follows: *knit to corner st, M1(see Techniques, page 103), k1, M1,* repeat around, ending with a M1, bind off last st. Cut yarn and fasten off carefully to create a smooth join.

Trivet Hanging Loop

(optional) Work as for hanging loop for Oven Mitt.

Finishing

Weave in loose ends on WS.

Bedroom Accents

Dress your dresser in felt with a tray, dresser scarf, eyeglass case, and jewelry bag. The dresser tray was really an unsuccessful attempt at making a trivet. I-cord proved to be a poor choice for an edging, making the piece cup into a bowl shape. For some reason the unfortunate trivet ended up on my dresser instead of in the reject box. Before long it had collected keys, change, and other odds and ends. Its real purpose was revealed! Remade in a different yarn, the transformed trivet was the building block for this complete set. It includes a dresser scarf that, unlike the more common lacy types, is a safe place to set a hot beverage.

Dresser Tray

Cast on 2 sts. Work back and forth in rows of garter st (knit every row) as follows:
Row 1: Knit.
Row 2: Inc in first st, k1—3 sts.
Row 3: Inc in first st, k2—4 sts.
Row 4: Inc in first st, knit to end of row.
Repeat Row 4, until there are 60 sts. Knit 2 rows even.
Next row: Ssk, knit to end of row. Repeat this row until 1 st remains. Do not cut yarn. Hold last stitch for border.

Border

Note: Pick up loops by slipping the smaller needle through one strand at the end of the garter ridges.
With spare smaller circular needle, pick up 28 loops along the first side edge (1 for each garter ridge), then 3 sts from corner, repeat for remaining 3 side edges, ending by picking up 2 loops from last corner next to the st on hold.
Place the st on hold onto the left point of the spare circular and cast on 2 more sts. Using working needle in your right hand, begin attached I-cord (see Techniques, page 103) as follows: K2, ssk, slip these 3 sts back onto

SIZES

Tray: *7½" (19 cm) square;* ***Dresser Scarf:*** *12½" by 24" (31.5 by 61 cm);* ***Eyeglass Case:*** *4" by 7½" (10 by 19 cm);* ***Jewelry Bag:*** *4½" by 5½" (11.5 by 14 cm).*

YARN

All items are made in DK-weight yarn. Worsted-weight may be substituted for slightly larger finished sizes. ***Tray:*** *120 yards (110 meters).* ***Dresser Scarf:*** *280 yards (256 meters) main color (MC), 60 yards (55 meters) of contrast color (CC).* ***Eyeglass Case:*** *65 yards (59.5 meters) main color (MC), 20 yards (18.5 meters) contrast color (CC).* ***Jewelry Bag:*** *65 yards (59.5 meters). Always test your yarns to be sure that they felt to a nice fabric at the gauge given.* ***Dresser Scarf and Tray*** *shown in Mannings Hawthorne Cottage English Leicester DK (100% wool; 189 yd [173 m]/3.5 oz): #32 (MC) and #303 Damson (CC). Tray requires 1 skein of CC. Scarf requires 2 skeins MC and 1 CC.* ***Jewelry Bag*** *shown in Classic Elite Lush (50% angora, 50% wool; 123 yd [112.5 m] 50 g): #4434 wine and #4457 lilac,1 skein per bag.* ***Eyeglass Case*** *shown in Bryspun kid-n-ewe (50% kid mohair, 50% wool; 120 yd [110 m] 50 g): #210 periwinkle (MC), 1 skein; and Hawthorne Cottage DK, #32 (CC), 1 skein.*

NEEDLES

Tray: *Size 10½ (6.5 mm) circular or straight needles. A spare 16" or 24" (40 or 60 cm) circular needle;* ***Dresser Scarf:*** *Size 10 (6 mm): 24" (60 cm) circular.* ***All other pieces:*** *Size 10 (6 mm), 16" (40 cm) circular. A spare 16" (40 cm) circular needle is needed for eyeglass case. Adjust needle size if necessary to obtain the correct gauge. Straight needles may be used for some of the pieces, but the circular needles are needed for the borders.*

NOTIONS

Markers; coilless pins for dresser scarf and eyeglass case; satin cord for jewelry bag drawstring; tapestry needle; waste cotton for jewelry bag.

GAUGE

Unfelted *Gauge is not critical for these patterns. The tray is knitted more loosely than the other pieces so it will felt to a thicker and firmer fabric.* ***Tray:*** *11 sts and 22 rows = 4" (10 cm) in garter stitch.* ***Jewelry Bag:*** *14 sts and 21 rows = 4" (10 cm) in Stockinette stitch (St st).* ***All other pieces:*** *12 sts and 24 rows = 4" (10 cm) in garter st.*
Felted ***Tray:*** *About 20 sts and 40 rows = 4" (10 cm).*
Jewelry Bag: *About 18 sts and 29 rows = 4" (10 cm).*
All other pieces: *About 16 to 18 sts and 32 to 36 rows = 4" (10 cm). Gauge will vary with the amount of felting and the shape of the item.*

FELTING

Follow basic felting instructions on page 10 for all pieces, felting until they are down to the desired size. The tray should be felted firmly to hold its shape.

left needle and repeat. Work around the edge in this manner until all sts have been worked off of the spare needle. Cut yarn and sew the 3 remaining sts to the 3 cast-on sts to finish.

Finishing

Weave in loose ends carefully, remembering that both sides of the tray will show.

Dresser Scarf

(see Materials, page 90)
With MC, work as for tray until there are 60 sts. Mark each end of last row with a pin or split marker. Work even in garter st for about 9" (23 cm). (Adjust this length for a longer or shorter scarf.) Mark each end of last row with a pin.

Dec Row: Ssk, knit to end of row. Repeat this row until 1 st remains. Cut yarn and fasten off. Join CC and beginning next to the last point, pick up and knit 1 st for each garter ridge along slanted edge, 3 sts close together at marked corner (keep the center st marked), 1 st for each ridge across straight side, 3 sts at next corner, 1 st for each ridge along the slanted edge, then 5 sts close together at cast-on corner. Repeat this sequence for the other half of scarf. Join and knit border in rounds.

Rnd 1: Purl.

Rnd 2: *Knit up to first marked corner, M1 (see Techniques, page 103), k1, M1, knit to next corner, M1, k1, M1, knit up to 2 sts from the end corner st, [M1, k1] 3 times, M1; repeat from * once more, k1.

Repeat rnds 1–2 once more (there will be 2 knit sts at the end of the knit rnd), then repeat rnd 1 once more. Bind off knitwise *and at the same time* work the increases at the corners as before.

Finishing

Weave in loose ends on WS.

Jewelry Bag

(see Materials, page 90)
Cast on 42 sts. Place marker and join, being careful not to twist sts. Work even in rnds of St st (knit every rnd) for 36 rnds or about 6½" (16.5 cm).

Eyelet rnd: *Yo, k2tog, k1; repeat from *—42 sts.

Knit 2 rnds. Purl 2 rnds. Bind off loosely, knitwise. Cut yarn and fasten off.

Finishing

Sew cast on edge together to close bottom of bag. Weave in loose ends on WS. Thread a length of waste cotton through the eyelets to hold them open during felting. When felted and dry, brush the surface lightly with a stiff bristled brush to bring up the angora. Cut out waste cotton and replace with satin cord or ribbon.

Eyeglass Case (see Materials, page 90)

With MC, cast on 16 sts. Work back and forth in garter st (knit every row) for 47 rows—24 garter st ridges.

Shape Top Edge

K10, wrap next st and turn (W&T) (see Techniques, page 103), k4, W&T, k6, W&T, k8, W&T, k10, W&T, k12, W&T, knit to end of row.

Inc row: K7, M1, k2, M1 (see Techniques, page 103), k7—18 sts. Cut MC.

Join CC and knit 4 rows. Bind off loosely knitwise. Leaving remaining st on needle, rotate work and pick up and knit 27 sts (1 st for each garter ridge) down the side, mark last st for corner, pick up and knit 16 sts from cast-on edge, then 28 sts along 2nd side edge, marking the first st for corner. Cut yarn, slip sts onto a spare circular needle and set aside. Make 2nd half the same, but do not cut yarn.

Lay first half RS down with 2nd half, RS up, on top.

With both needles in your left hand, work a 3-needle join (see Techniques, page 103), checking that corner sts match.
Next row: Knit up to first marked st, M1, k1, M1, knit to next corner, M1, k1, M1, knit to end.
Turn and bind off loosely knitwise, and *at the same time* work M1 increases on each side of corner sts as in previous row. Cut yarn and fasten off.

Finishing

Weave in loose ends on WS.

Personal Comfort

Sometimes nothing feels better than a hot pack on tired aching muscles. Some of us reach for a flaxseed- or rice-filled microwave pack, and others find comfort with an old-fashioned hot water bottle. No matter what your preference is, you can have a comfy, colorful felt cover for your hot pack or hot water bottle.

Neck Cozy

This cozy is just large enough to cuddle your neck. You may choose to make your cozy wider or longer by adjusting the stitch count and/or length to center.

Loosely cast on 54 sts. Place marker and join, being careful not to twist sts. Knit in rnds of St st (knit every rnd) for about 13" (33 cm).

Center Opening and Under Flap

K24, turn, cast on 1 st, p22 sts (counting the cast on st), turn.
Cast on 1 st, k23, (counting the cast on st).
Working only on these 23 sts, turn, and beginning with a purl row, work 10 rows of St st (knit on RS, purl on WS).
Next Row: Bind off 23 sts loosely. Cut yarn and fasten off.
Cast 17 sts onto the right needle, then knit around remaining 33 sts on needle—50 sts.
Rejoin work into rnd and knit around to marker.
Inc rnd: K7, M1 (see Techniques, page 103), [k3, M1] 3 times, knit to end of rnd—54 sts.
Knit even in rnds of St st for an additional 13" (33 cm), or to match first half. Turn work inside out. Slip half the stitches onto a spare needle, and work a 3-needle bind-off (see Techniques, page 103). Cut yarn and fasten off.

Finishing

Sew cast-on edges together to close the other end.

SIZES
Neck Cozy: About 5" by 21" (12.5 by 53.5 cm). ***Bottle Cover:*** *10" by 14" (25.5 by 35.5 cm). The st count may be adjusted to accommodate other sizes.*

YARN
Light to medium worsted-weight yarn. ***Neck Cozy:*** *230 yards (210.5 meters).* ***Bottle Cover:*** *300 yards (274.5 meters). Always test your yarns to be sure that they felt to a nice fabric at the gauge given. The neck cozy is shown in Mountain Colors Mountain Goat (55% mohair, 45% wool; 240 yd [219.5 m] 4 oz): yellowstone, 1 skein. The hot water bottle cover is shown in Classic Elite Lush (50% angora, 50% wool; 123 yd [112.5 m] 50 g): #4434 wine, 3 skeins.*

NEEDLES
Neck cozy: *Size 10 (6 mm), 16" (40 cm) or 24" (60 cm) circular and spare 24" (60 cm) circular.* ***Bottle cover:*** *Size 10 (6 mm), 24" (60 cm) circular. Adjust needle size if necessary to obtain the correct gauge.*

NOTIONS
Markers; fine waste cotton thread for basting; 18" [46 cm] of waste cotton to thread through eyelets of bottle cover while felting; silk ribbon to thread through eyelets of bottle after felting; 2"–3" (5–7.5 cm) of Velcro if desired; ½ yard (46 cm) muslin fabric for neck cozy insert; flaxseed or rice for filling neck cozy insert; tapestry needle.

GAUGE
Unfelted *14 sts and 21 rows = 4" (10 cm) in Stockinette st (St st) for both items.*
Felted *About 18–20 sts and 26–28 rows = 4" (10 cm). Gauge will vary with the amount of felting and is not critical for these patterns.*

FELTING
Follow basic felting instructions on page 10, felting to desired size. Since the neck cozy is a long narrow piece, it will be prone to stretching and/or twisting while felting, especially during the first stages. To counteract this tendency, straighten and pull into shape each time you do a progress check.

On inside, slip-stitch the side edges of under flap to bag. Weave in loose ends on WS. Using a fine cotton thread, loosely baste the opening closed. If desired, after bag is felted and dry, sew Velcro in place at center opening.

Making the Inside Bag

Using the finished felted cover as a pattern, cut a piece of muslin the length of the bag and twice as wide. Do not add for seam allowances because the inner bag should be slightly smaller than the cover. Seam the long edge and one short edge. Fill with flaxseed or rice to desired fullness (don't overfill) and sew the remaining end closed. Insert inner bag in the cover.
To use, microwave on medium power for 30 seconds at a time till you reach desired warmth. Do not overheat.

Hot Water Bottle Cover

You may have seen a luxury-fiber hot water bottle cover offered through an exclusive catalog for several hundred dollars. Not to be outdone, I chose an angora blend for my luxury cover. If you are more the woolly type, substitute any wool that will felt to about the same gauge.

Loosely cast on 90 sts. Place marker and join, being careful not to twist sts.
Knit in rnds of St st (knit every rnd) for 85 rnds or about 16" (40.5 cm).
Dec rnd: *K1, k2tog; repeat from *—60 sts.
Knit 2 rnds even.
Eyelet rnd: *Ssk, k1, yo; repeat from *. Knit 22 rnds even in St st. Change to garter st (purl 1 rnd, knit 1 rnd) for 5 rnds, ending with a purl rnd. Bind off loosely knitwise. Cut yarn and fasten off.

Finishing

Sew cast-on edges together to close bottom of bag. Weave in loose ends on WS. Thread a length of waste cotton through the eyelets to hold them open during felting. When felted and dry, brush the surface lightly with a stiff bristled brush to bring up more angora. To maintain an air of luxury, thread a matching silk ribbon through the holes after the cover is felted and dried.

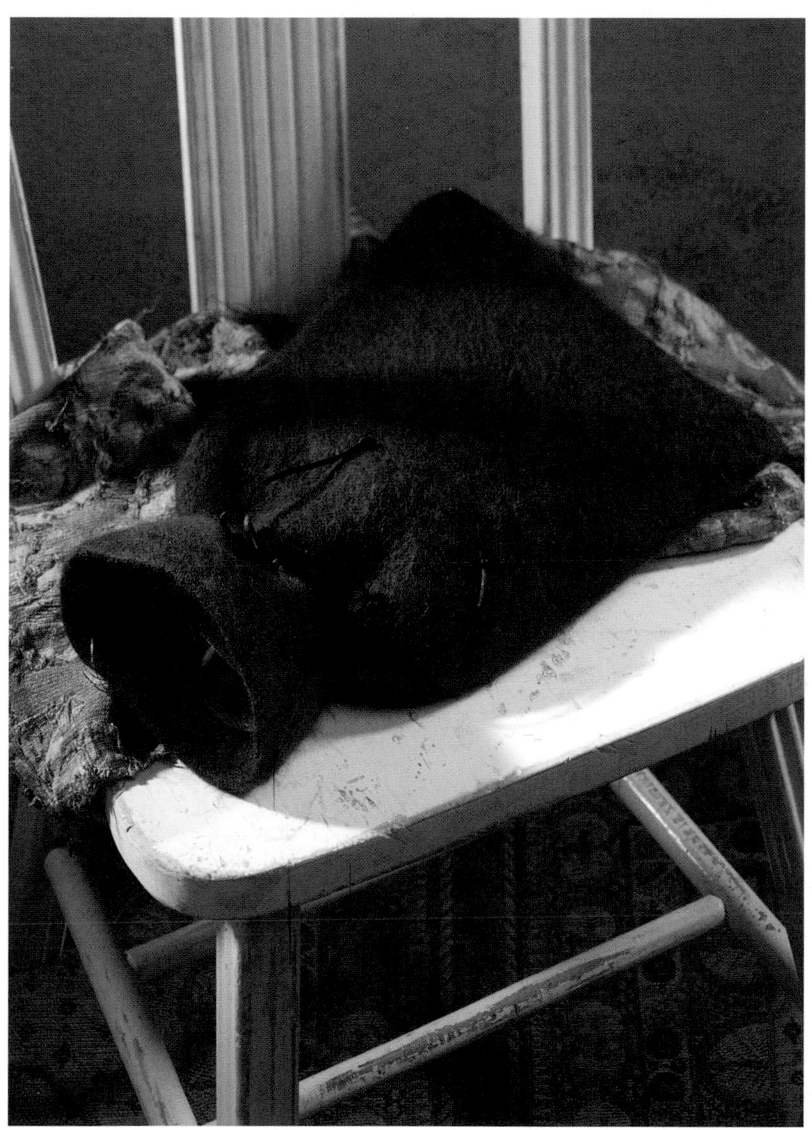

needle felting

Needle felting is a fun and easy way to embellish your felted knits. Using felting needles and spare yarn or fiber you can add lettering or small motifs as shown here or create a complex, one-of-a-kind, work of art on a pillow or vest. It's like painting with fiber.

FELTING NEEDLES

A felting needle is a fine, very sharp, barbed needle. Mounted in beds of thousands, these needles are used by textile mills to manufacture many types of commercial non-woven fabrics. Felting needles do their work without water. When the needle is stabbed into the wool, the barbs catch small amounts of the surface fiber, carrying them down and locking them into the fibers below. Since the barbs only catch in one direction, the more you stab, the more tightly the fibers are locked.

Felting needles come in many sizes or gauges. The smaller the gauge number, the larger (coarser) the needle. A 36-gauge needle will bond fibers faster, but will also leave visible puncture holes. These needles are best used only for initial felting work. A 38-gauge needle is a good all-purpose size, and a 40-gauge needle is used for a smooth finish.

Many different styles of felting needles are available. The triangle-point with 3 barbed sides, and the star-point with 4 barbed sides are the most common. The extra barbs on the star-point needles will bond fibers much more quickly.

MATERIALS FOR NEEDLE FELTING

Fibers for needle-felted embellishment may come from many sources. Consider using yarn from your scrap bag as well as fleece, batting, or roving. Yarn may be used as is or pulled apart into wisps of fiber to smoothly cover an area or to blend colors. Even synthetic yarns and fibers may be used and are worth trying.

KYU

In addition to your fiber you'll need felting needles in assorted gauges. You'll also need a piece of cushion foam that's roughly 6" long by 8" wide (15 by 20.5 cm) and at least 2" (5 cm) thick. This foam protects your work surface as well as the tips of the needles. You can also use an old pillow or a thick sponge if you don't have a piece of foam. If you are working on a finished item such as a bag or pair of mittens you'll want a piece of foam that fits inside your felted item. The foam prevents the needle-felted fibers from being carried into the other side of your piece.

APPLYING THE FIBER

A great way to start is by needle felting a small sample design on one of your test swatches or trial projects.

Place your felt swatch on the foam and lay a piece of fiber or yarn on top of it. (Yarn may be used as is or pulled apart into wisps of fiber.) Give the fiber a few stabs with your needle to get a feel for how it works. Stab the needle straight in and just deep enough so that the barbs pass through the fiber and the felt. Stabbing too deeply will just carry fibers down into your foam. Continue by adding a few more pieces of fiber and stabbing them a few times until they are stuck to the felted item. At this point, if you don't like how things are looking, you can easily pull the fibers off and reposition.

Once you like your design, begin stabbing (or needling) repeatedly, all over the design fibers, to permanently bond them to the felt. Remember not to stab too deeply! Lift your work off the foam occasionally to be sure you are not pushing the fiber into it. Add more fiber as you work. Be sure to use tweezers or some other tool when fibers need to be pushed, pulled, or rearranged. When the design is securely attached, and you're satisfied with it, change to a finer needle for finishing the surface.

For a really smooth surface, try wet-felting the finished design. Dip your hand in a bowl of water into which you've added a small amount of Woolmix or other rinse-free wool wash. Rub the solution briskly into the surface of your design, adding more water as needed, but not soaking the piece. You want just enough moisture to smooth the top layer for a nice finish.

EXAMPLE 1: LETTERING

The lettering on the little gift bag shown on page 97 is quick and easy. Here's how to do it.

First, cut very short pieces of hand-dyed yarn and arrange them in the letter shape, stabbing each piece a couple of times to tack it on. Once you like the way all the letters look, stab the yarn a few more times to attach it firmly, then began adding additional little wisps of fiber pulled from the yarn. Using small amounts of yarn fluff will give you more control over the colors and a smoother finished surface than if you use whole strands of yarn.

EXAMPLE 2: SHEEP

Using some scraps of wool batting, shape the woolly sheep's body into a rough oval before placing it on the bag. Then, using a double-pointed needle to hold the edges in place, tack the sheep onto the bag with stabs of the felting needle. Once the edges are secured in the shape you want, needle it all over to permanently bond it to the bag. For my sheep (shown on page 97) I added small pieces of black fleece for the face, feet, and tail and tacked them in place. I rearranged and added to them, until my little sheep had the proper personality, then I needled repeatedly until bonded. I added more fiber to any thin spots and finished with a 40-gauge needle.

WHAT ELSE CAN YOU DO WITH A FELTING NEEDLE?

You can mend your felt slippers or mittens! If you find a spot is wearing thin and have saved some yarn (a good idea), just cut some short pieces, pull them into fluff, and begin needling it in place. Add more fluff as needed to bring the worn spot back to the original thickness and your slippers will be as good as new.

You can also use needle felting to make and decorate anything from felted Easter eggs to intricate dolls and animals. Check your bookstore or library for books with instructions. With your felting needles and some wool, the possibilities are endless!

CAUTION

Sharp Points!

Felting needles are very sharp and the tiny barbs make for a painful puncture if you stab your finger. Keep your eyes on the work and your fingers out of the way. A pair of tweezers or a short knitting needle make good tools for moving and holding the fiber in place, and keeping your fingers safe. Felting needles are brittle. Do not use them as tools for moving or rearranging the fiber as they are likely to break. When not in use, store the needles in their protective sleeves safely out of the reach of children.

felting notes for yarns

This is not intended to be a complete list of good yarns for felting, just a few personal favorites. It would take pages to list all possible yarn choices, and new ones come on the market every season. Always be ready to grab your needles and make a small sample project to try out new, or new to you yarns that look interesting.

Baabajoes Wool Co.

Woolpak NZ, 100% New Zealand Wool

All colors of this yarn are fast and easy to felt, *including the natural white.* Available in three weights, 8-ply (DK), 10-ply (worsted), and 14-ply (bulky), Woolpak can be used for nearly all felting projects and it felts quickly.

Blue Sky Alpaca

Alpaca Sport and Alpaca Bulky, 100% Alpaca

Available in a range of rich colors, Blue Sky Alpaca felts to a beautiful, soft fabric.

Brown Sheep Co.

Burley Spun, 100% Wool

I tried this yarn for the first time when I was working on the rug for this book and I was thrilled with the results. Being super bulky-weight, it's much too thick to lose stitch definition even when felted. When I worked the yarn in garter stitch, however, the resulting stitch definition added interesting texture to the rug.

Hand Paint Originals, 70% Mohair, 30% Wool

This quick-felting, hand-painted yarn is a great choice for adding both color and mohair to your felted knits. It's perfect for small areas of trim; otherwise it's best used with another yarn. Used alone, it can be a bit hard to handle, felting thicker than you may want, or felting together where it shouldn't. I frequently combine it with Nature Spun or Lamb's Pride worsted.

Lamb's Pride, 85% Wool, 15% Mohair

Available in either worsted-or bulky-weight,

guidelines

- Remember that bleached white is not recommended for felting in any yarn.
- Unless noted otherwise, be cautious of naturals and any light, clear colors.
- Heather colors often take a long time to felt and may not shrink as much as solid colors, but the end result is often a very nice pliable fabric.
- Always test-felt in the color you are planning on using.

Lamb's Pride felts well, is widely available, and comes in an unbeatable 70-color palette. The mohair adds a slight, but not overpowering, halo to the finished felted fabric.

Nature Spun, 100% Wool
Nature Spun is a good, basic, worsted-weight felting yarn that can be used alone (either single- or double-stranded) to create a smooth felted fabric. Since it's not too heavy, it's one of my favorite choices for combining with a strand of mohair or novelty yarn.

Bryspun Yarns
kid-n-ewe, 50% Wool, 50% Mohair
Used single-stranded, kid-n-ewe felts to a soft fabric suitable for baby items, berets, and soft bags. Use it double-stranded or combine it with another yarn to thicken the fabric. Kid-n-ewe is available in 65 wonderful colors.

Cascade Yarns
Cascade 220, 100% Wool
Cascade is a good all-purpose worsted-weight wool for making a smooth felted fabric or blending with other yarns such as mohair or novelty.

Classic Elite
Lush, 50% Angora, 50% Wool
This yarn felts to a sturdy fabric with a wonderful luxurious feel.

Montera, 50% Llama, 50% Wool
Montera felts very easily to a thick, fuzzy fabric.

Dale of Norway
Heilo, 100% Norwegian Wool
Heilo is an excellent choice for a firm, smooth felted fabric. Being a double knitting (DK) weight, it makes a smaller felted gauge than most worsted-weights.

Garnstudio
Angora Tweed, 70% Merino Wool, 30% Angora
This yarn is somewhat slow to felt, but worth the wait. Angora Tweed creates a very soft fabric with a beautiful halo of angora. Some stitch definition may show under the angora, but it does not distract from the look. Not sturdy enough for items like slippers that will see hard wear, it's a good choice for a baby hat or a soft evening bag.

Green Mountain Spinnery

Double Twist, 100% Wool

This yarn may feel somewhat coarse in the hank, but felting transforms it into a soft, pliable fabric. Double Twist is not too heavy, so it is a good choice for berets and soft bags.

Green Mountain 2-ply, 100% Wool

Green Mountain 2-ply is similar to Double Twist, but it seems to felt to a slightly heavier fabric. The rag tweed-type colors create a heathered fabric.

Mountain Mohair, 70% Wool,
30% Yearling Mohair

A favorite for slippers, hats, and bags, Mountain Mohair is best used with a strand of wool. The soft yearling mohair gives the felted fabric a fuzzy halo, which can be brushed to an almost furry look.

Mountain Colors

Mountain Goat, 55% Mohair, 45% Wool
4/8's Wool, 100% Wool

These are two of my favorite felting yarns from Mountain Colors' sublime palette. Mountain Goat and 4/8's Wool are available in a wide range of unique, hand-painted colorways.

SR Kertzer Naturally Yarns

Tussock, 85% New Zealand Wool,
15% Polyester

Tussock is available in 8-ply (DK) or 10-ply (worsted) weight and felts quickly and easily. The polyester tweed strand adds both color and texture to a felted fabric.

techniques

Standard Bind-Off

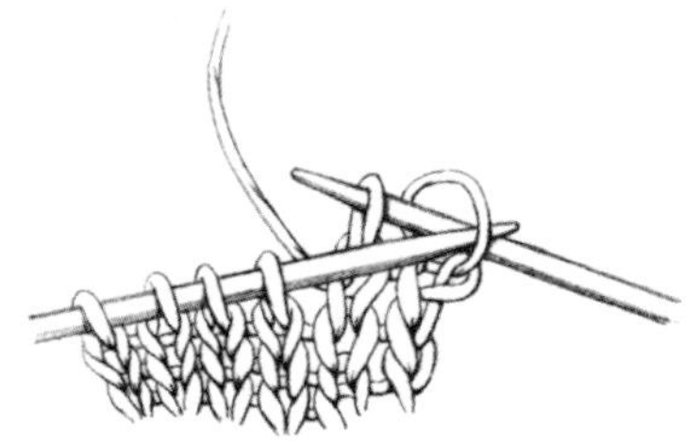

Figure 1

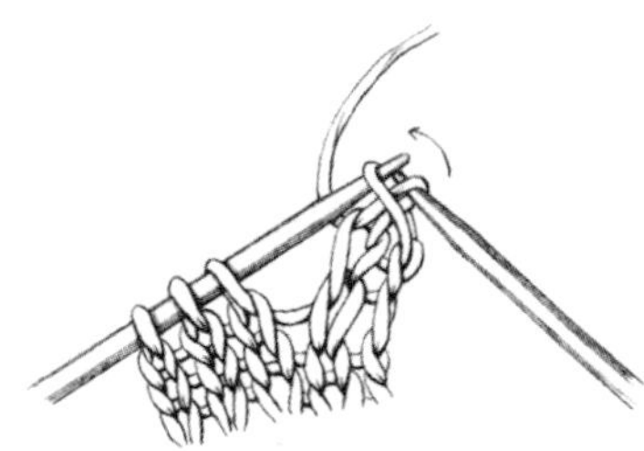

Figure 2

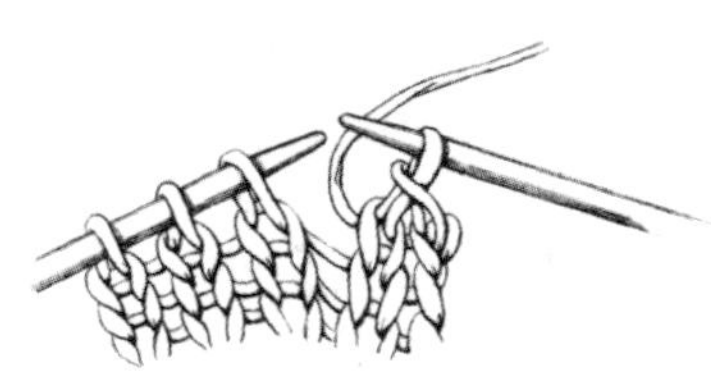

Figure 3

This is the most common, and for many knitters, the only method for binding off. Use this method for edges that will be sewn into seams or finished in some way (such as stitches being picked up and knitted). Slip 1 stitch, *knit 1 stitch, insert left needle tip into first stitch on right needle (Figure 1), pass this stitch over the second stitch (Figure 2), and off the needle—1 stitch remains on right needle and 1 stitch has been bound off (Figure 3). Repeat from *.

Mid-Row Bind-Off

Knitters find there are many times when they have to BO stitches in mid-row . . . working necklines, armholes, buttonholes, special details, and such. Counting the stitches for each section is sometimes confusing. *It's important to remember that it takes two stitches to BO one stitch.* If you forget this, you may find the stitch count in some sections of your work doesn't match those stated in the instructions.

Let's suppose our instructions tell us to k14, BO 12, k14. If you knit 14 sts then BO 1, the first section will be short two stitches. You'll have 12 knit stitches before the first BO. If you k15 and then BO 1, the first section will have 13 sts before the first BO. **In order to maintain** the correct number of stitches in each section, k14, *then knit two more stitches* . . . the first of which will be the first BO stitch.

After completing the BO, *don't forget the stitch remaining on the right needle is part of the next section* . . . in our example, the last 14 stitches. If you count the stitches on the left needle, there will only be 13, because the first stitch has been worked and is waiting on the right needle. **Work each section carefully**, counting the stitches worked before starting the next section.

3-Needle Bind-Off

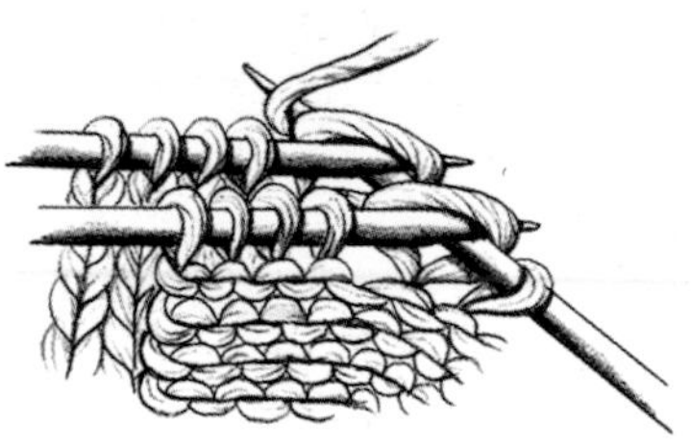

Place stitches to be joined onto two separate needles. Hold them with right sides of knitting facing together. *Insert a third needle into first stitch on each of the other two needles and knit them together as one stitch. Knit next stitch on each needle the same way. Pass first stitch over second stitch. Repeat from * until one stitch remains on third needle. Cut yarn and pull tail through last stitch.

3-Needle Join

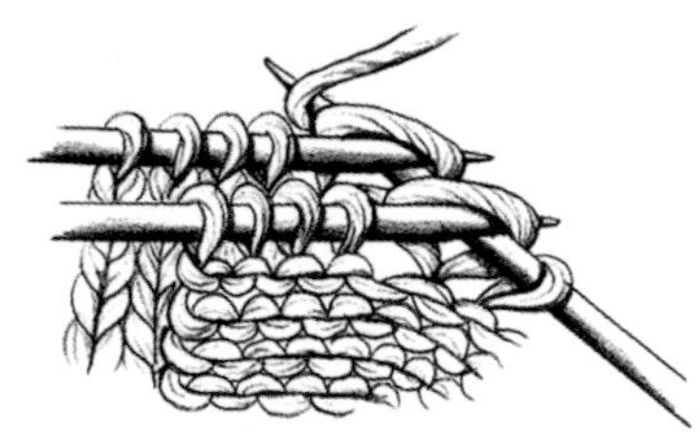

Place stitches to be joined onto two separate needles. Hold them with right side of knitting facing. *Insert a third needle into first stitch on each of the other two needles and knit them together as one stitch. Knit next stitch on each needle the same way. Repeat from * until all stitches have been knit.

I-Cord

With dpn, CO desired number of stitches. *Without turning the needle, slide stitches to other end of needle, pull yarn around back to front of needle, and knit the stitches as usual; repeat from * for desired length.

Crochet Chain (Provisional) Cast-On

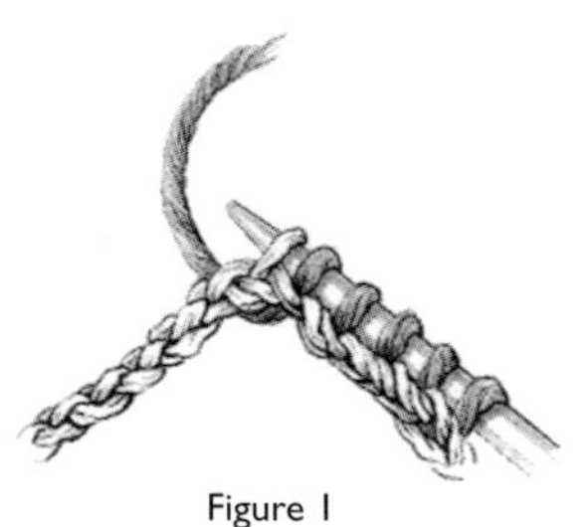

Figure 1

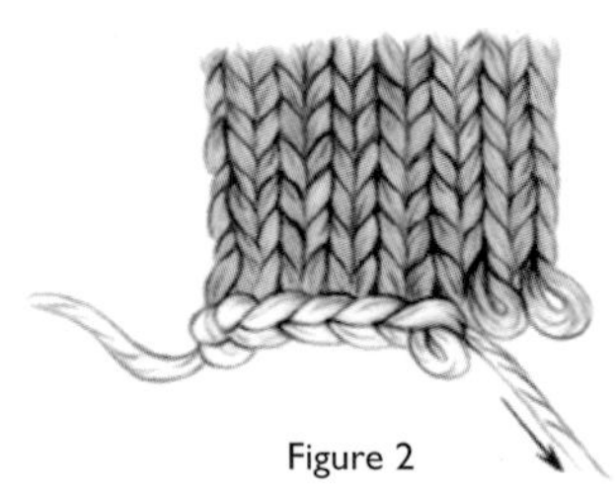

Figure 2

Make a crochet chain 4 stitches longer than the number of stitches you need to cast on. Pick up and knit stitches through back loops of the crochet chain. Pull out the crochet chain to expose live stitches when you're ready to knit in the opposite direction.

Make 1 (M1) Increase

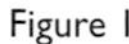
Figure 1

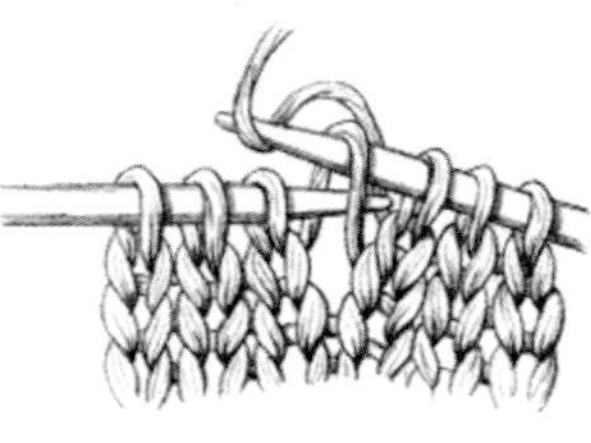
Figure 2

With left needle tip, lift the strand between last stitch and the first stitch on left needle, from front to back (Figure 1). Knit the lifted loop through back to close up the stitch (Figure 2). Makes a left slant increase without using adjacent stitches.

M1 Pwise Increase

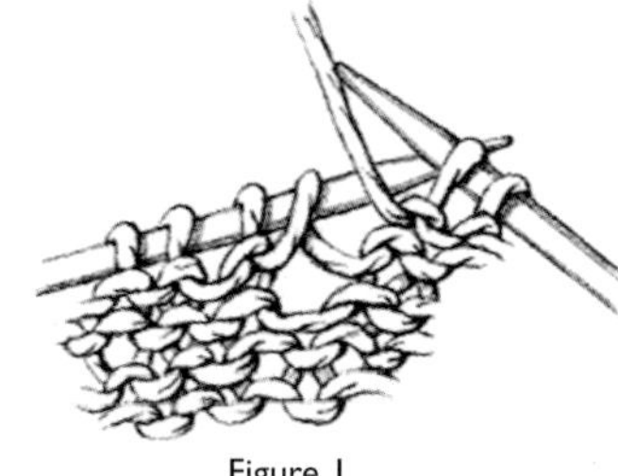
Figure 1

Figure 2

With left needle tip, lift the strand between the last knitted stitch and the first stitch on the left needle, from back to front and place on left needle (Figure 1). Purl the lifted loop (Figure 2).

K2tog Decrease

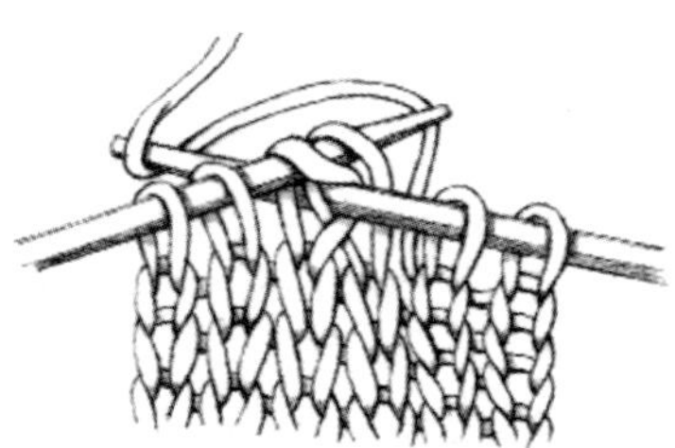

A single, right-slanting decrease. On right side rows, knit two stitches together as if they were a single stitch.

Short Row with Wrap and Turn (W&T)

Figures 1 and 2

Work short rows as directed up to the turning point (the W&T).

Knit St: If the last stitch was a knit, work the W&T as follows:
1. Slip the next stitch (purlwise) onto the right needle.
2. Bring yarn forward between the needles.
3. Return slipped stitch to left needle.

Figure 3

4. Turn to work in the opposite direction, moving the yarn back between the needles if the next stitch is a knit or leaving the yarn in front to purl.

Purl St: If the last stitch was a purl, work the W&T as follows:
1. Slip next stitch (purlwise) onto the right needle.

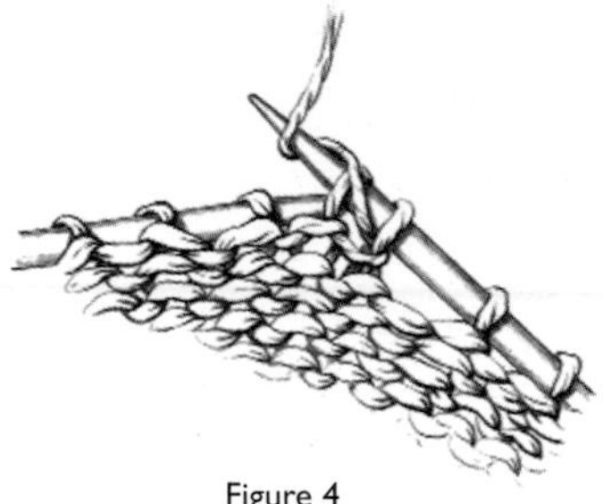
Figure 4

2. Take the yarn to the back between the needles.
3. Return slipped stitch to left needle.
4. Turn to work in the opposite direction, bringing the yarn to the front between the needles if the next stitch is a purl, or leaving it in back to knit.

SSK Decrease

Figure 1

Figure 2

This is a left slanting decrease. Slip two stitches, one at a time, as if to knit (Figure 1). Insert the point of the left needle, from left to right, into the front of these two stitches. Knit them together from this position (Figure 2).

Sewing a Zipper In

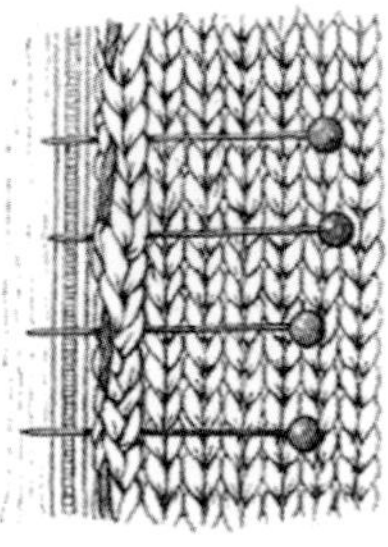
Figure 1

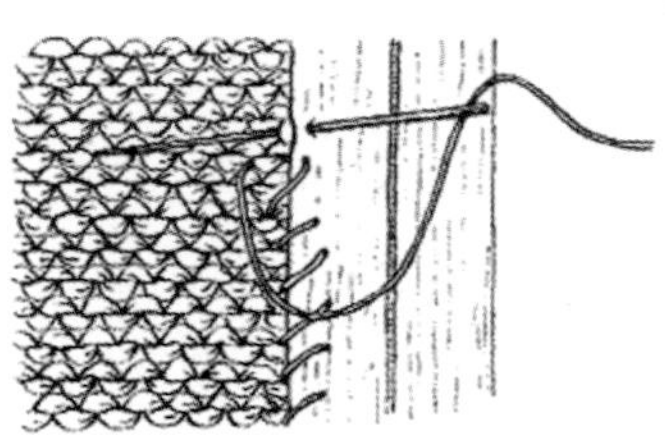
Figure 2

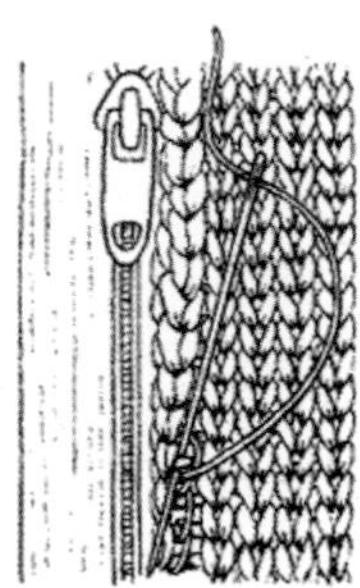
Figure 3

Zippers are an excellent choice when a plain closure is in order.

Working from the right side and beginning at the base, pin each side of the closed zipper to the wrong side of the felted fabric so the edges of the knitting come together and hide the teeth. Take care to keep the zipper flat and at the same position on both sides. With contrasting thread, baste the zipper in place close to the teeth (Figure 1).

Remove the pins. Turn the work over and use coordinating thread to whipstitch the edges of the felted fabric (Figure 2), making sure that the stitches do not show on the right side. Turn the work back to the right side. With coordinating thread and using a backstitch, sew the felted fabric to the zipper close to the teeth (Figure 3).

Readers with access to a sewing machine may prefer to use one. We used a machine to sew the zippers to the vests in this book.

Using a "stitching in the ditch formed by the border" method proved a very successful way to insert a zipper. Whatever the method you choose, always preshrink the zipper first, before attaching.

Flat Seam

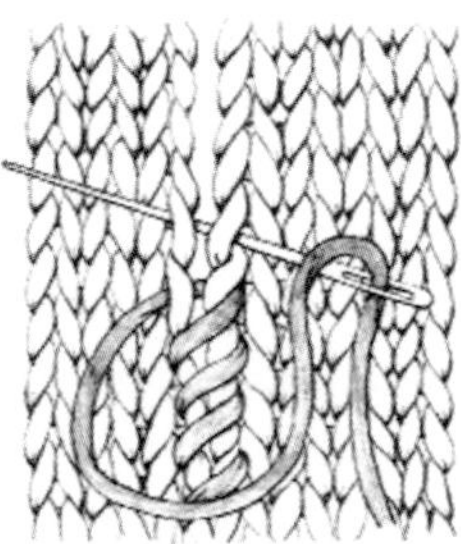

Place both garment pieces to be seamed on a flat surface, with RS facing up. Using the project yarn threaded on a sharp needle, working upwards, catch the edge stitch on one piece then the edge stitch on the other piece. Keep the sewing tension loose and the seam flat. You can also use the same method with WS together and the seam edges pinned. Use the same overcast-style sewing stitch on the RS as the flat method. Open this seam flat when finished.

abbreviations

cm	centimeter(s)
CC	contrast color
dec	decrease(s)
dpn	double-pointed needle(s)
g	gram(s)
k	knit
k2tog	knit 2 sts together
inc	increase(s)
M 1	make 1 st. See Techniques.
m	meter(s)
M	marker(s)
MC	main color
mm	millimeter(s)
oz	ounce(s)
p	purl
pwise or purlwise	as if to purl
p2tog	purl 2 sts together
rnd(s)	round(s), as in circular knitting
RS	right side
kwise or knitwise	as if to knit
ssk	a left-slant decrease. Slip 2 stsone at a time kwise from the left needle to right needle, insert left needle tip into front loops of both sts and knit them together through their back loops.
st(s)	stitch(es)
W&T	wrap and turn, used in short rows, see Techniques.
WS	wrong side
yd	yard(s)
*	repeat starting point (i.e., repeat from *)
*	repeat all instructions between asterisks
( )	alternate measurements and/or instructions
[ ]	instructions that are to be worked as a group a specified number of times.

sources

WHOLESALE SUPPLIERS My thanks to the following wholesale yarn companies who provided materials for the projects in this book. Please look for their products at your local yarn store.

Anny Blatt USA
7796 Boardwalk
Brighton, MI 48116
www.annyblatt.com
Angora Super

Aurora Yarns
PO Box 3068
Moss Beach, CA 94038
(650) 728-2730
Garnstudio Angora Tweed

Baabajoes Wool Co.
PO Box 260604
Lakewood, CO 80215
www.baabajoeswool.com
Baabajoe's Woolpak 10-ply and 14-ply

Berroco, Inc.
14 Elmdale Rd.
Uxbridge, MA 01569
www.berroco.com
info@berroco.com
Jewel FX, Zapp

Blue Sky Alpacas, Inc.
PO Box 387
St. Francis, MN 55070
(888) 460-2198
www.blueskyalpacas.com
Blue Sky Alpaca sportweight

Brown Sheep Co.
100662 Cty. Rd. 16
Mitchell, NE 69357
(308) 635-2198
www.brownsheep.com
Burleyspun, Hand Paint Originals, Lamb's Pride worsted and bulky, Naturespun

Bryson Distributing
4065 West 11th Ave. #39
Eugene, OR 97402
www.brysonknits.com
kid-n-ewe

Cascade Yarns
PO Box 58168
Tukwila, WA 98138
www.cascadeyarns.com
Cascade 220

Classic Elite Yarns, Inc.
300 Jackson St.
Lowell, MA 01852
Lush, Montera

Dale of Norway
N16 W23390 Stoneridge Dr., Ste A
Waukesha, WI 53188
(800) 441-DALE (3253)
www.daleofnorway.com
Ara, Heilo

Green Mountain Spinnery
PO Box 568
Putney, VT 05346
(800) 321-9665
www.spinnery.com
Mountain Mohair, Green Mountain Double Twist worsted and 2-ply

S. R. Kertzer and Naturally Yarns
105A Winges Rd.
Woodbridge, ON
Canada L4L 6C2
(800) 263-2354
www.kertzer.com
Fizz, Naturally Tussock 10-ply

Mountain Colors
PO Box 156
Corvallis, MT 50828
(406) 777-3377
Mountain 3-ply, Mountain goat

Trendsetter Yarns
16745 Saticoy #101
Van Nuys, CA 91406
trndstr@aol.com
Sorbet

Wholesale Needle Felting Supplies, Suede Slipper Soles and Mitten Palms
Please look for these products at your local yarn store.

Fiber Trends
PO Box 7266
East Wenatchee, WA 98802
(509) 884-8631
www.fibertrends.com

RETAIL SUPPLIERS

My very special thanks to these retailers who answered my last-minute pleas for more yarn.

Acorn Street Shop
2818 N.E. 55th St.
Seattle, WA 98105
(206) 525-1726
(800) 987-6354
www.acornstreet.com

The Mannings
1132 Green Ridge Rd.
PO Box 687
East Berlin, PA 17316
(717) 624-2223
(800) 233-7166
www.the-mannings.com
Hawthorne Cottage Yarns

BUTTON SUPPLIERS

The Button Shoppe
4744 Oakfield Cir.
Carmichael, CA 95608
(916) 488-5350
(888) 254-6078
www.buttonshoppe.com

Ellen's Half Pint Farm
85 Tucker Hill Rd.
Norwich, VT 05055
(802) 649-5420
www.ellenshalfpintfarm.com

bibliography

Armes, Jean Paccagnan. *Felted Treasures.* West Vancouver, British Columbia: Self published, 2002.

Fournier, Nola, and Jane Fournier. *In Sheep's Clothing.* Loveland, Colorado: Interweave Press, 2003.

Nabney, Janet. *Machine Knitted Fabrics: Felting Techniques.* London: B. T. Batsford Ltd., 1993.

Sparks, Patricia. *Fundamentals of Feltmaking.* Petaluma, California: Unicorn Books & Crafts, 1989.

Talpai, Ayala. *The Felting Needle.* Marcola, Oregon: Diligence Woodwork & Design, 2000.

Thomas, Mary. *Mary Thomas's Knitting Book.* New York: Dover Publications, 1972.

Vickrey, Anne Einset. *The Art of Feltmaking.* New York: Watson-Guptill Publications, 1997.

index